CONFIGURING ACCOUNTS RECEIVABLE WITHIN DYNAMICS AX 2012

BY MURRAY FIFE

ISBN: 1501080776

ISBN-13: 978-1501080777

Preface

What You Need For This Guide

All the examples shown in this blueprint were done with the Microsoft Dynamics AX 2012 virtual machine image that was downloaded from the Microsoft CustomerSource or PartnerSource site. If you don't have your own installation of Microsoft Dynamics AX 2012, you can also use the images found on the Microsoft Learning Download Center or deployed through Lifecycle Services. The following list of software from the virtual image was leveraged within this guide:

- Microsoft Dynamics AX 2012 R3

Even though all the preceding software was used during the development and testing of the recipes in this book, they may also work on earlier versions of the software with minor tweaks and adjustments, and should also work on later versions without any changes.

Errata

Although we have taken every care to ensure the accuracy of our content, mistakes do happen. If you find a mistake in one of our books—maybe a mistake in the text or the code—we would be grateful if you would report this to us. By doing so, you can save other readers from frustration and help us improve subsequent versions of this book. If you find any errata, please report them by emailing editor@dynamicsaxcompanions.com.

Piracy

Piracy of copyright material on the Internet is an ongoing problem across all media. If you come across any illegal copies of our works, in any form, on the Internet, please provide us with the location address or website name immediately so that we can pursue a remedy.

Please contact us at legal@dynamicsaxcompanions.com with a link to the suspected pirated material.

We appreciate your help in protecting our authors, and our ability to bring you valuable content.

Questions

You can contact us at help@dynamicsaxcompanions.com if you are having a problem with any aspect of the book, and we will do our best to address it.

Table Of Contents

INTRODUCTION

The Accounts Receivable area is one of the three foundation financial modules within Dynamics AX that you will want to set up. It not only allows you to manage all of your customer information, post your invoices, and receive in your cash payments, but also allows you to manage your collections, track deductions, and much more.

It's not hard to configure either and this book is designed to give you step by step instructions to show you how to configure the receivables area, and also how some of the basic transactions work to get you up and running and working with your customers.

CONFIGURING ACCOUNTS RECEIVABLE CONTROLS

Before we start adding customers and creating invoices within the Accounts Receivable module of Dynamics AX, there are a couple of codes and controls that need to be configured so that everything else later on in the book will run smoothly. In this section we will walk through everything that you need to set up to get the basic Accounts Receivable features working.

Configure Receivables Journal Names

Everything you do within the Receivables area of Dynamics AX is controlled through Journals. So it makes sense that the very first thing that we need to do is to configure some default Journal Names that we can then start using for our journal postings. We will want to create two new Journals right now for Customer Payments and also Write-Offs.

Configure Receivables Journal Names

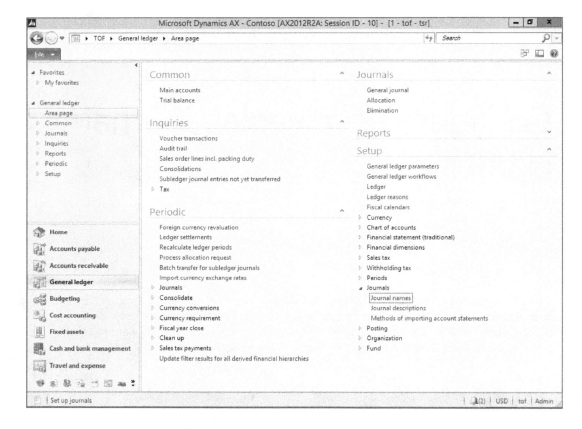

To do this, click on the **Journal Names** menu item within the **Journals** folder of the **Setup** group within the **General Ledger** area page.

Configure Receivables Journal Names

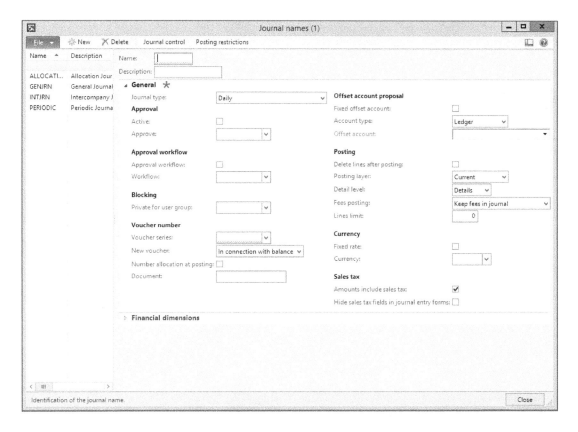

When the **Journal Names** maintenance form is displayed, click on the **New** button in the menu bar to create a new record.

Configure Receivables Journal Names

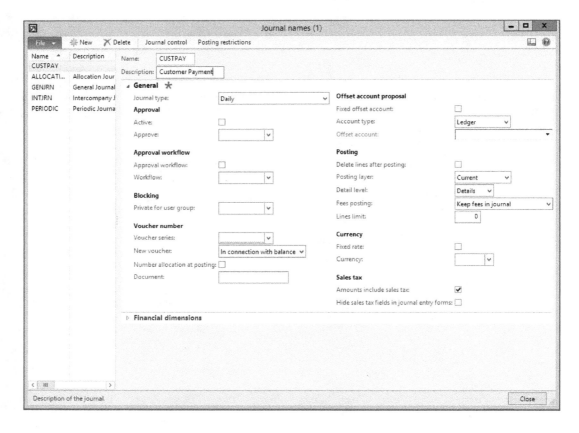

For the first Journal, set the **Name** to **CUSTPAY** and the **Description** to **Customer Payment**.

Configure Receivables Journal Names

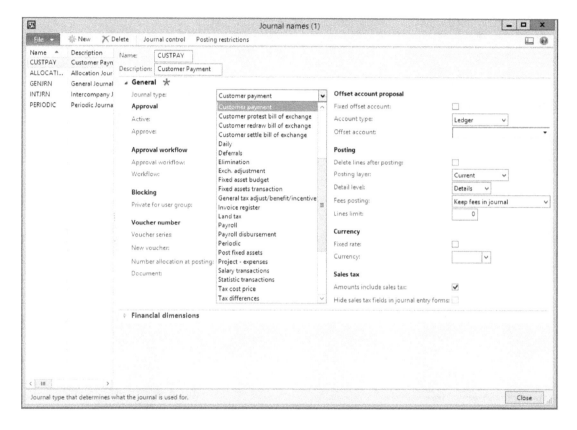

Then click on the **Journal Type** dropdown list box and select the **Customer Payment** value.

Configure Receivables Journal Names

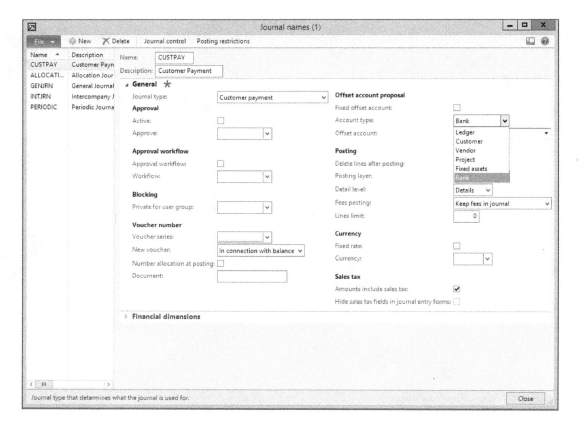

Within the **Offset Account Proposal** field group, click on the **Account Type** dropdown box and select the **Bank** option to identify that the journal will be posting to the bank accounts by default.

Configure Receivables Journal Names

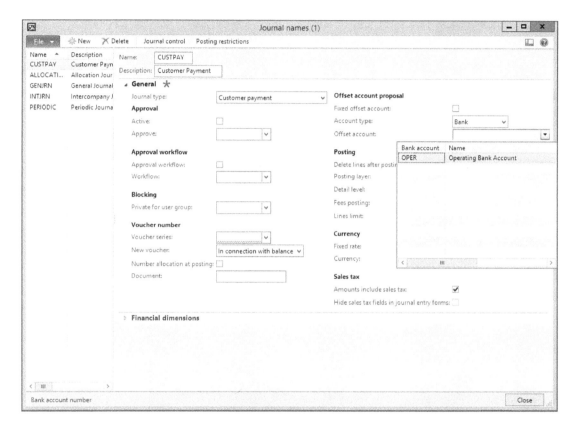

Then from the **Offset Account** dropdown, select the **Bank Account** that you want the customer payment to post to.

Configure Receivables Journal Names

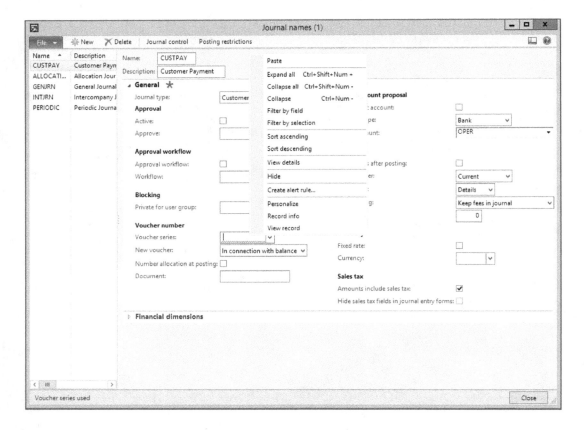

Now we need to give out Journal a number sequence. We don't have one right now, so we will create one by right-mouse-clicking on the **Voucher Series** field and selecting the **View Details** option.

Configure Receivables Journal Names

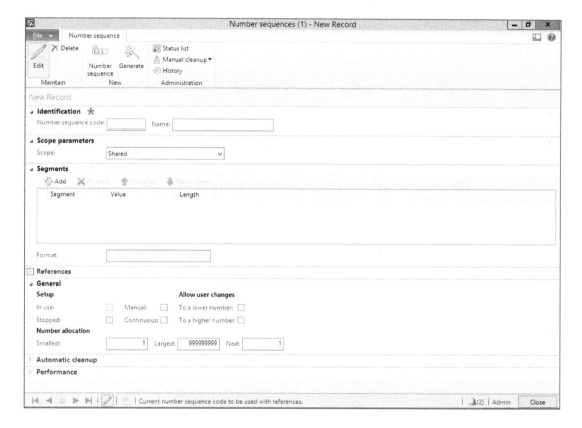

When the **Number Sequence** maintenance form is displayed, click on the **Number Sequence** button within the **New** group of the **Number Sequence** ribbon bar.

Configure Receivables Journal Names

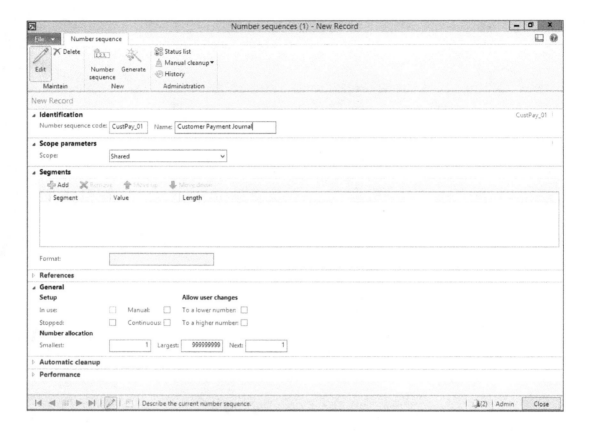

Give your number sequence a **Number Sequence Code** and a **Description.**

Configure Receivables Journal Names

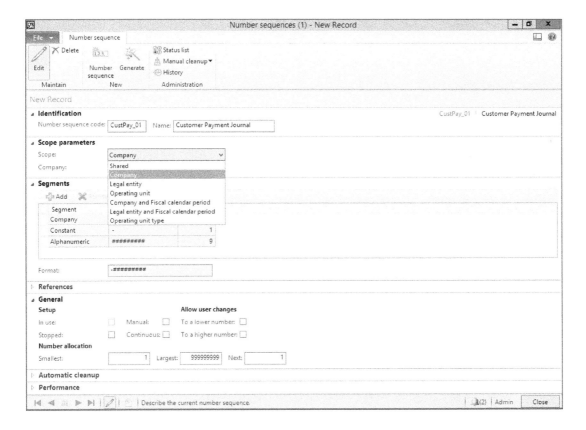

Then set the **Scope** to **Company** to identify that this number sequence only belongs to one organization.

Configure Receivables Journal Names

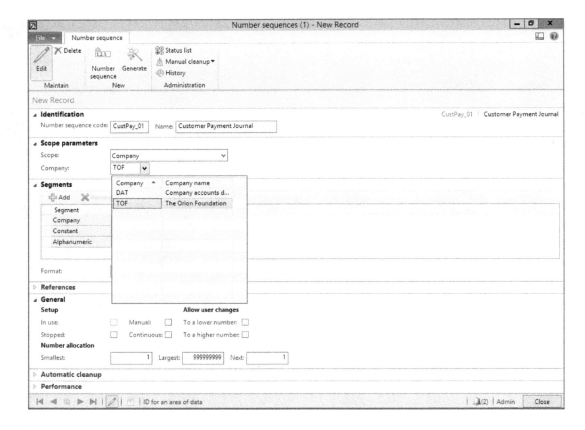

And from the **Company** dropdown list, select your primary company.

Configure Receivables Journal Names

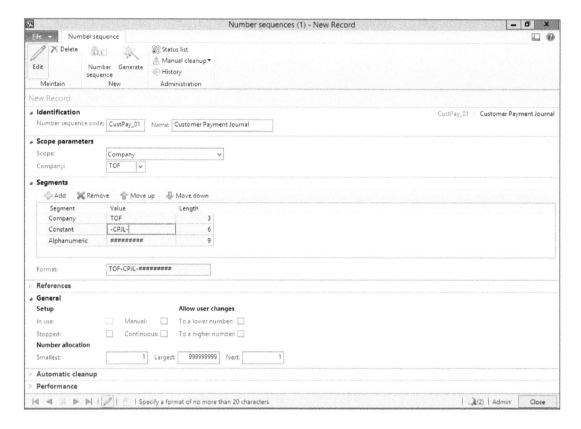

Tweak the **Segment** structure to include the **Company** and also add a unique **Constant** value that will allow you to recognize that these postings are customer payments.

Configure Receivables Journal Names

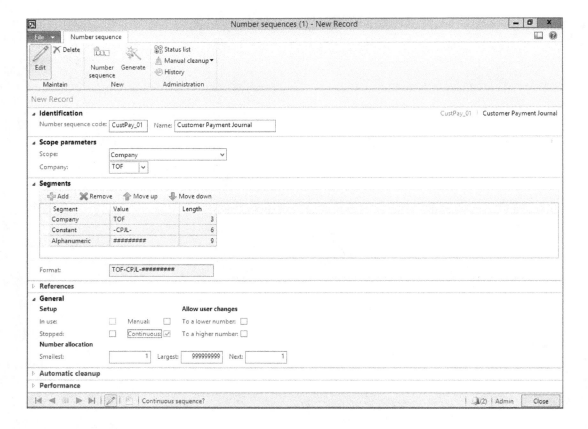

Then set the **Continuous** flag within the **General** tab group.

When you have done that, click on the **Close** button to exit from the form.

Configure Receivables Journal Names

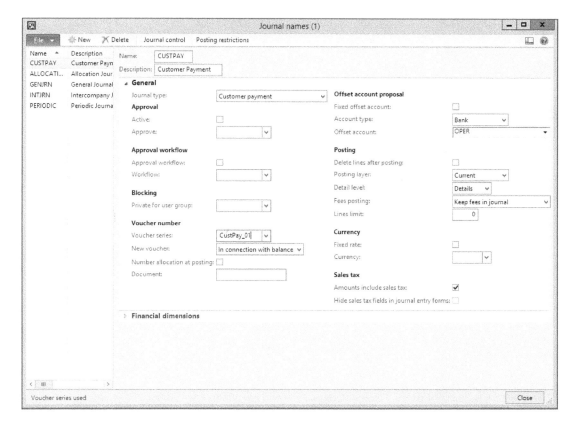

When you return back to the Journal Names form you will be able to select your new Number but Sequence from the **Voucher Series** dropdown list.

Configure Receivables Journal Names

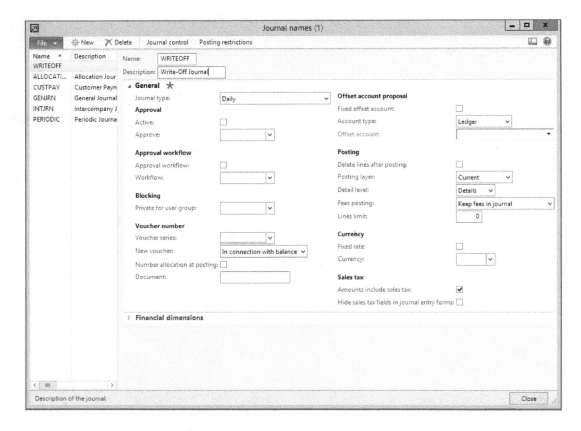

We will add one more Journal Name for a Write-Off by clicking on the **New** button in the menu bar, and then setting the **Name** to **WRITEOFF** and the **Description** to **Write-Off Journal**.

Configure Receivables Journal Names

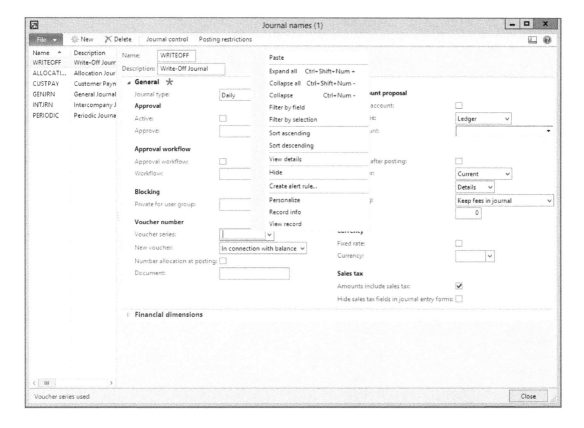

Right-mouse-click on the **Voucher Series** field and select the **View Details** menu item.

Configure Receivables Journal Names

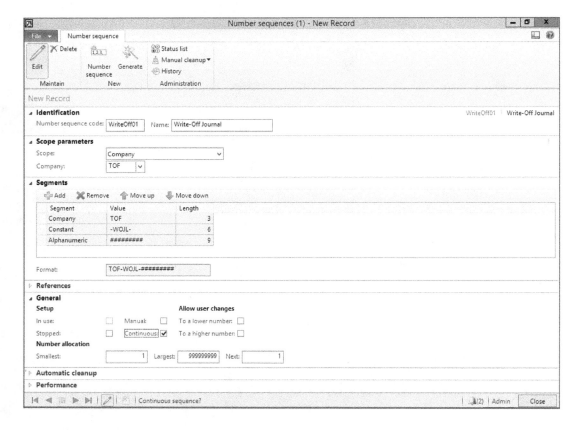

And create a new number sequence for the journal just the same way as you created the Customer Payment number sequence and then click on the **Close** button to exit from the form.

Configure Receivables Journal Names

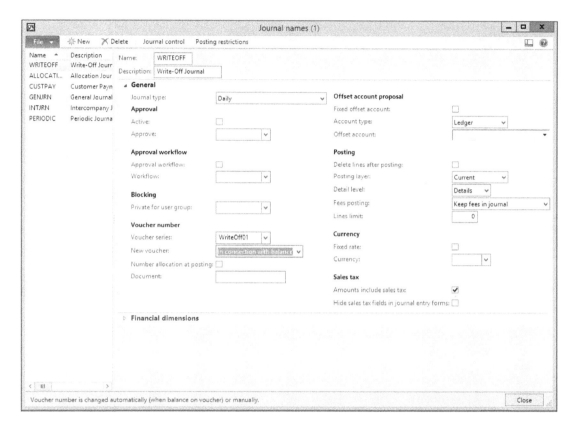

When you return back to the **Journal Names** form, assign your Write-Off journal the new Voucher Series, and then click on the **Close** button to exit from the form.

Configuring Customer Posting Profiles

The next setup task that we will need to perform is to configure a set of default **Posting Profiles** for the Receivables area. These are used to default in common posting accounts and configurations for all, or groups of customers. We will want to create two of these profiles initially, one for our General postings, and another for Pre-payments.

Configuring Customer Posting Profiles

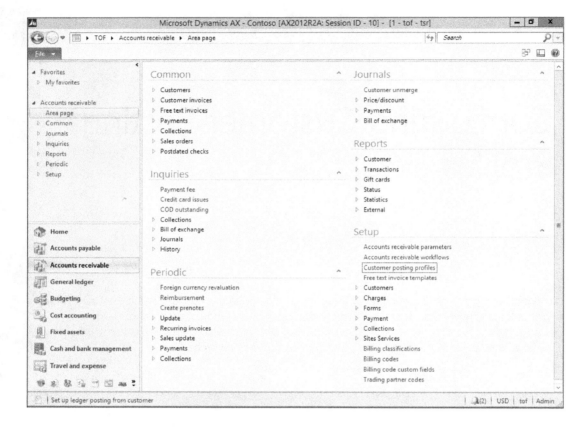

To do this, click on the **Customer Posting Profiles** menu item within the **Setup** group of the **Accounts Receivable** area page.

Configuring Customer Posting Profiles

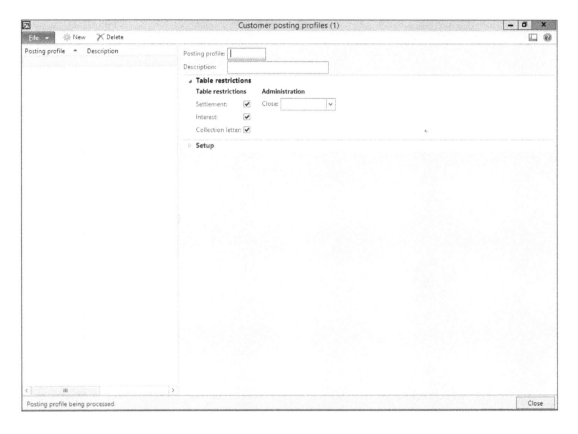

When the **Customer Posting Profiles** maintenance form is displayed, click on the **New** button in the menu bar to create a new record.

Configuring Customer Posting Profiles

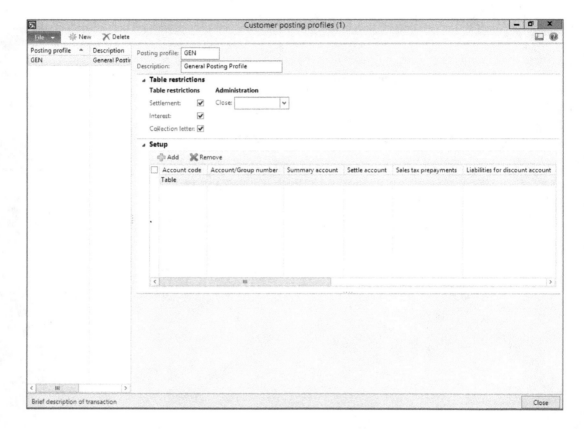

Set the **Posting Profile** code to be **GEN** and the **Description** to **General Posting Profile**.

Configuring Customer Posting Profiles

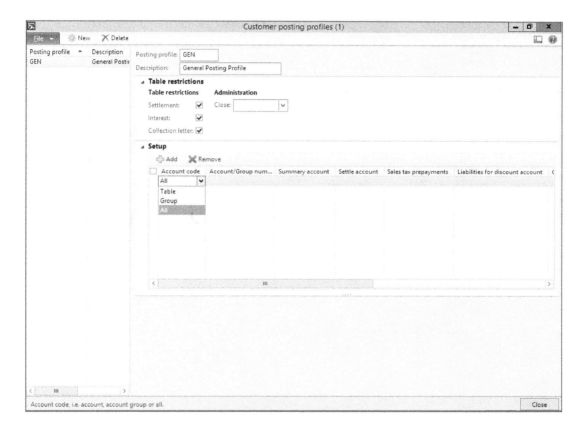

Then within the **Account Code** dropdown list within the **Setup Table** select the **All** option.

Note: Notice that there is also an option for **Group** (which will allow you to create a posting profile for a group of customers) and **Table** (which will allow you to create a posting profile specific to an individual customer).

Configuring Customer Posting Profiles

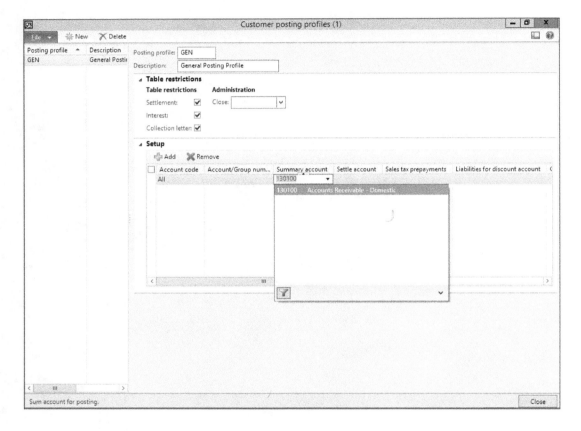

Then select a main account from the **Summary Account** field dropdown.

Configuring Customer Posting Profiles

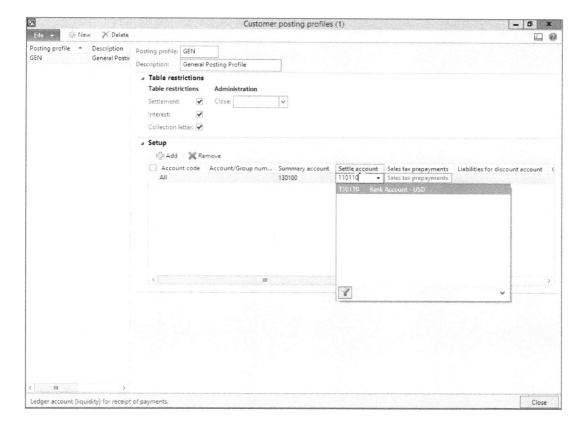

Then select the main account that you want to post to when settling transactions. In this case we will post to the bank account.

Configuring Customer Posting Profiles

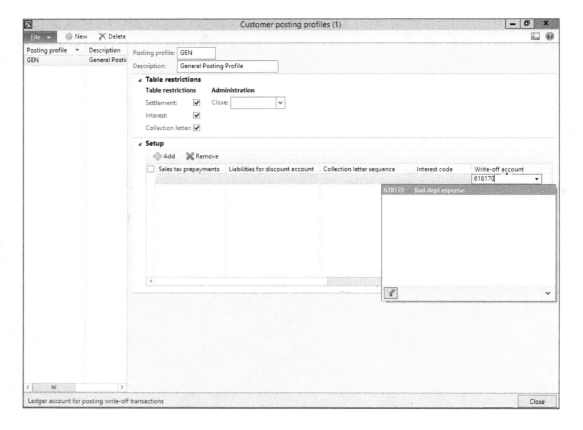

Finally, select a **Write-Off Account** to post our write-off transactions to.

Configuring Customer Posting Profiles

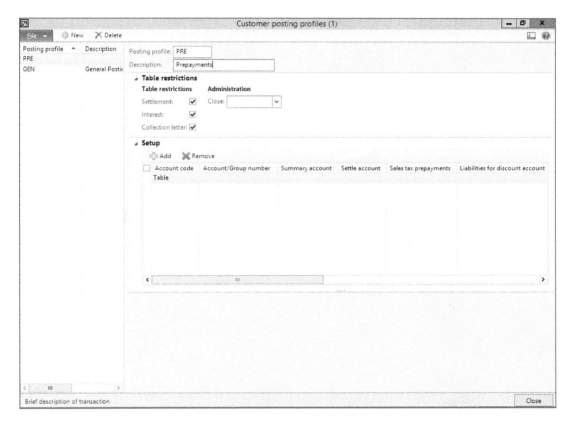

Then click on the **New** button in the menu bar to create our second **Customer Posting Profile** record and give it a **Posting Profile** code of **PRE** and a **Description** of **Prepayments/**

Configuring Customer Posting Profiles

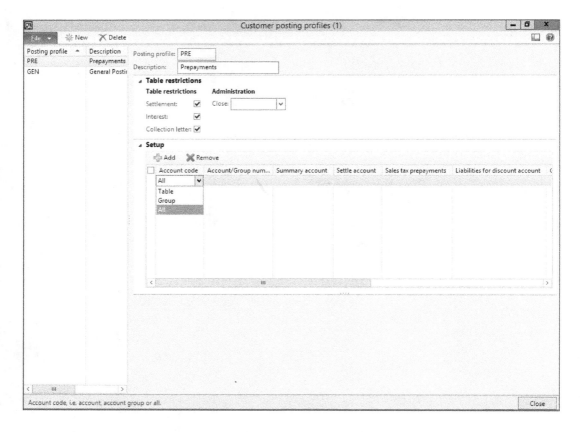

Within the **Setup** grid, set the **Account Code** to **All.**

Configuring Customer Posting Profiles

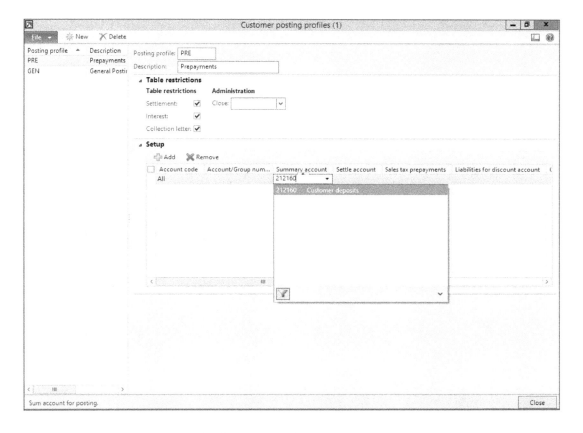

Set the **Summary Account** to a holding account for the pre-payments.

Configuring Customer Posting Profiles

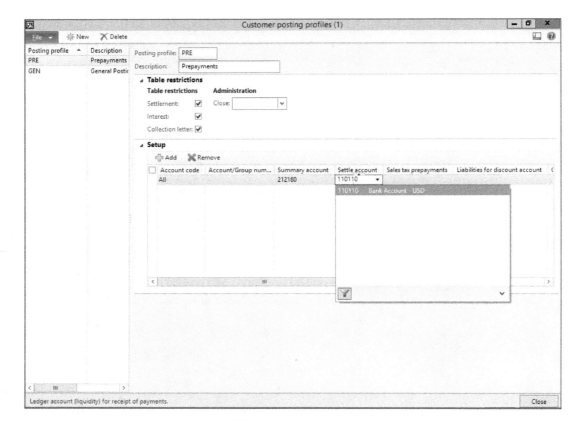

Set the **Settle Account** field to point to our bank accounts main account.

Configuring Customer Posting Profiles

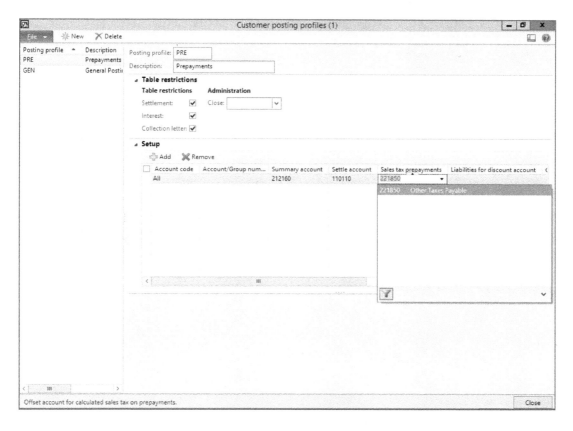

And if you are going to be tracking sales tax, specify a **Main Account** for the **Sales Tax Prepayments** field.

Configuring Customer Posting Profiles

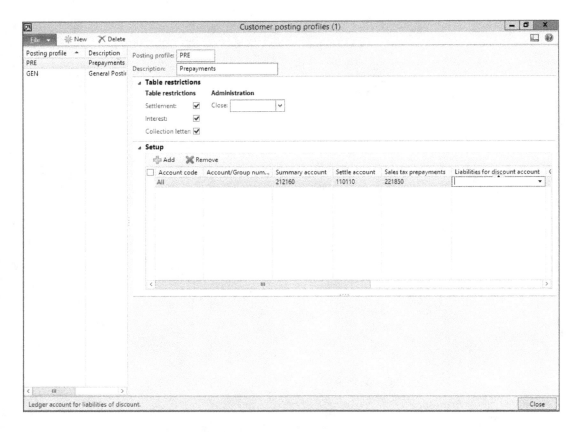

When you have done that you can just click the **Close** button and exit from the form.

Configuring Cash Payment Terms

Now we can start configuring some of the codes and controls to manage your cash receipts. The best place to start with this is to configure your **Cash Payment Terms** so that you can assign them to your customer accounts later on.

Configuring Cash Payment Terms

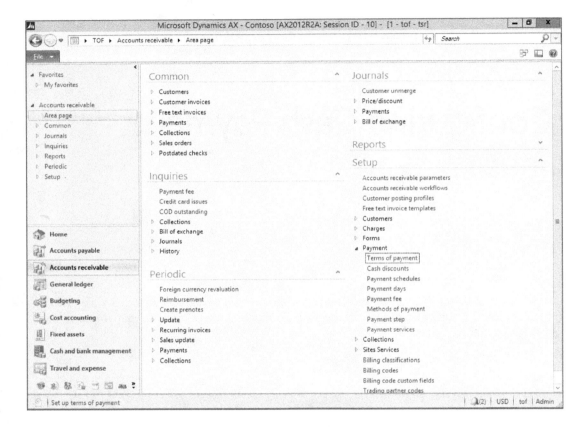

To do this click on the **Terms Of Payment** menu item within the **Payment** folder of the **Setup** group within the **Accounts Receivable** area page.

Configuring Cash Payment Terms

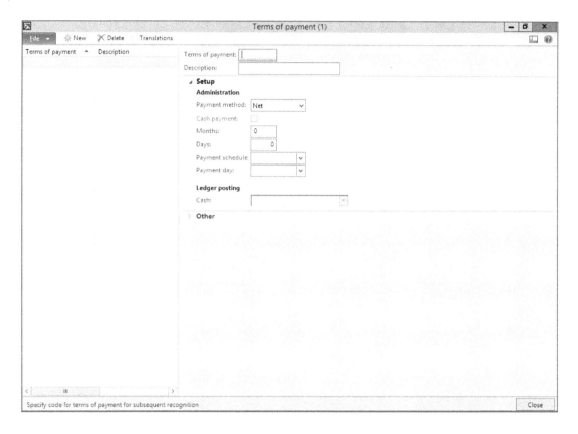

When the **Terms of Payment** maintenance form is displayed, click on the **New** button in the menu bar to create a new record.

Configuring Cash Payment Terms

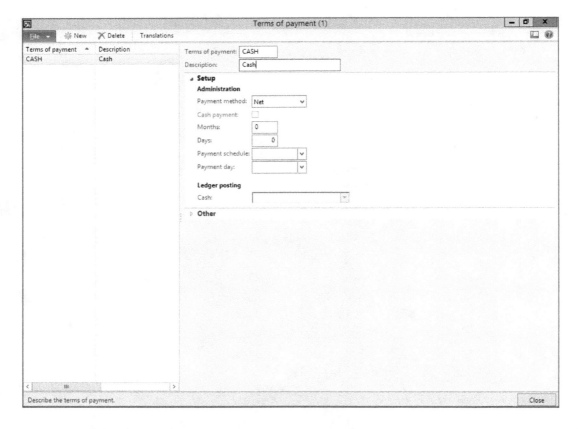

First we will create a **Cash** payment term. To do this, set the **Terms of Payment** to **CASH** and set the **Description** to **Cash**.

Configuring Cash Payment Terms

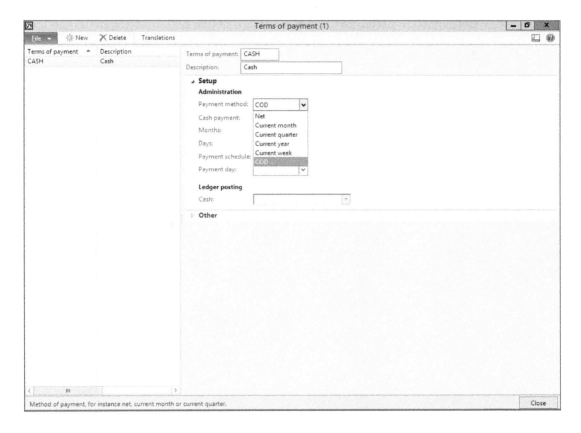

From the **Payment Method** dropdown list, select the **COD** option.

Configuring Cash Payment Terms

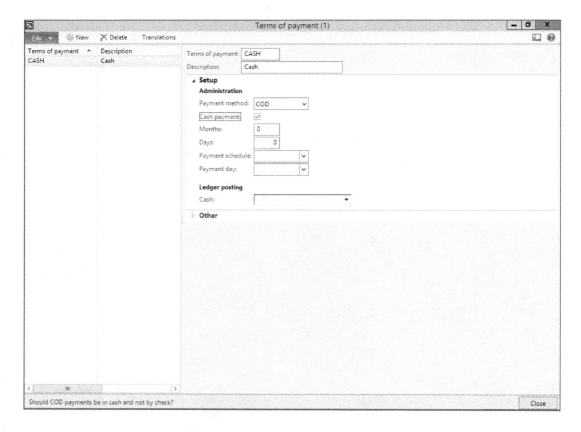

Then check the **Cash Payment** option flag.

Configuring Cash Payment Terms

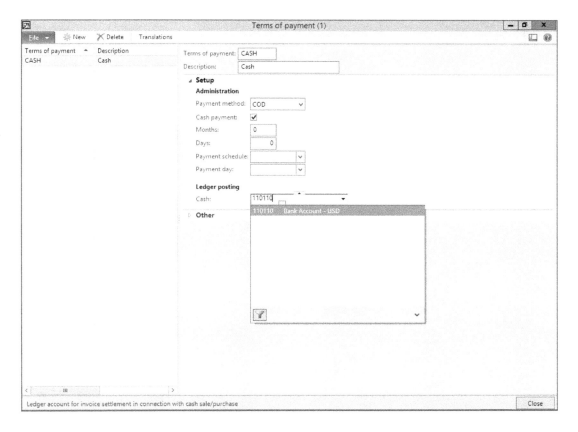

Finally, within the **Ledger Posting** field group, select the main account that you want to post to from the **Cash** field dropdown list.

Configuring Cash Payment Terms

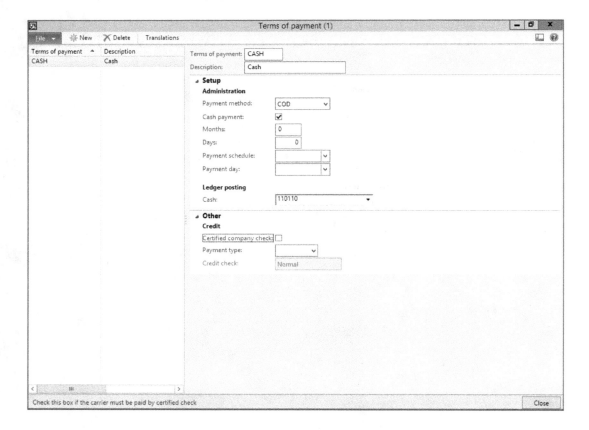

Configuring Cash Payment Terms

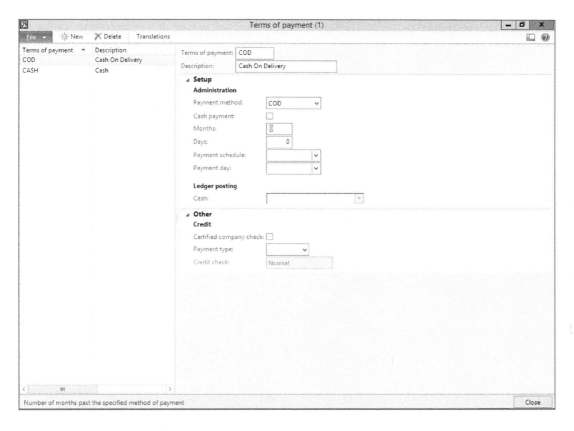

You can also create a **Cash On Delivery** Terms of Payment as well. The only difference with this record is that you do not need to check the **Cash Payment** flag.

When you are done, you can click on the **Close** button to exit from the form.

Configuring Net Days Payment Terms

Another type of Payment Term that you may want to configure is a Net Days Payment to pay on or before the date.

Configuring Net Days Payment Terms

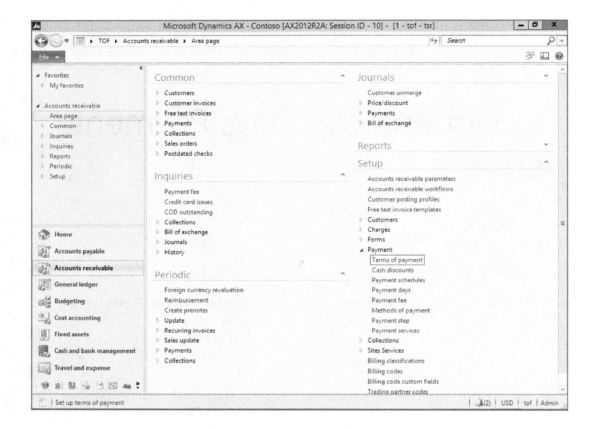

To do this click on the **Terms Of Payment** menu item within the **Payment** folder of the **Setup** group within the **Accounts Receivable** area page.

Configuring Net Days Payment Terms

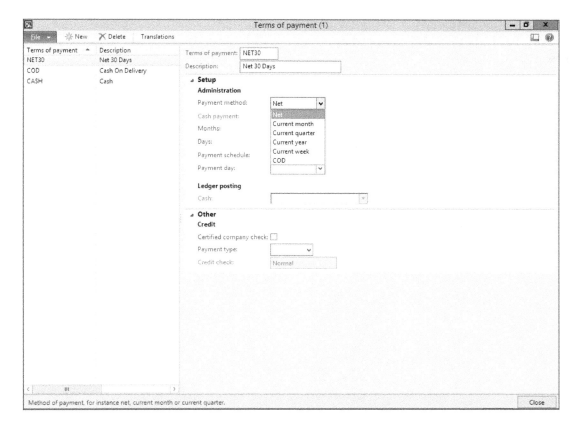

When the **Terms of Payment** maintenance form is displayed, click on the **New** button in the menu bar to create a new record.

Set your **Terms Of Payment Code** to **NET30**, and set the **Description** to **Net 30 Days**.

Then from the **Payment Method** dropdown list, select the **Net** option.

Configuring Net Days Payment Terms

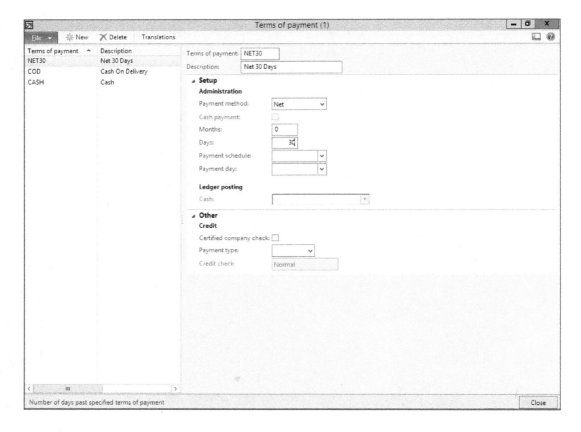

Within the **Days** field, set the number of days to **30**.

Configuring Net Days Payment Terms

You can continue adding additional variations of the Net Payment Terms until you have all of the different options for your customers, and then click the **Close** button to exit from the form.

Configuring Net Day Of Month Payment Terms

Another type of Payment Term that you may want to offer to your customers is the option to pay on a certain day of the month. This requires a little additional configuration, but is still not a big deal.

Configuring Net Day Of Month Payment Terms

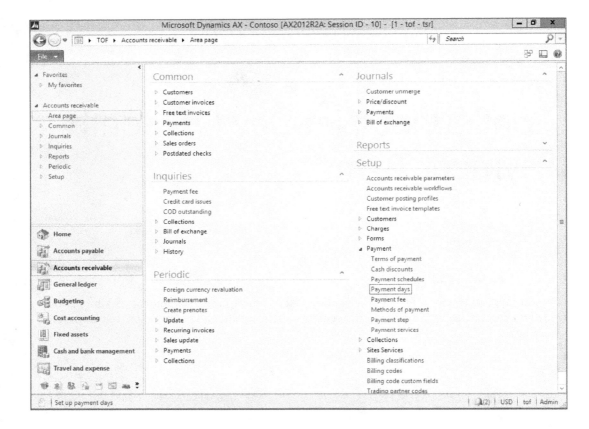

For this type of Payment Term you first need to configure the days that you want to allow. To do this, click on the **Payment Days** menu item within the **Payment** folder of the **Setup** group within the **Accounts Receivable** area page.

Configuring Net Day Of Month Payment Terms

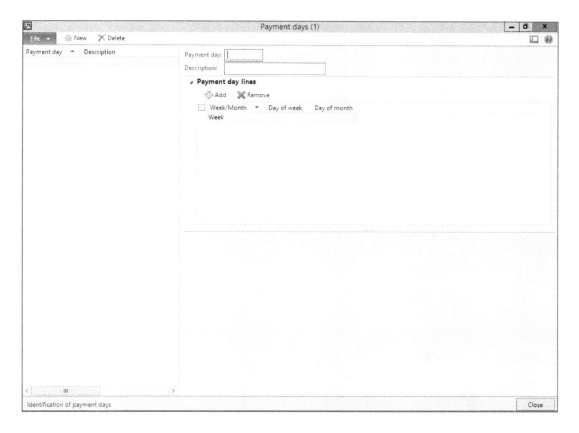

When the **Payment Days** maintenance form is displayed, click on the **New** button to add a new record.

Configuring Net Day Of Month Payment Terms

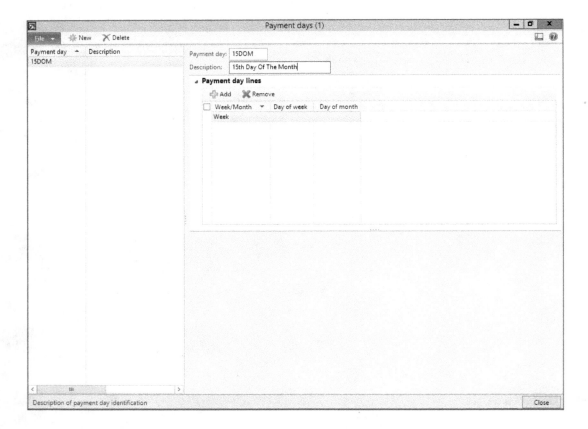

Set the **Payment Day** field to **15DOM**, and the **Description** to **15th Day Of The Month** to start defining mid-month payment terms.

Configuring Net Day Of Month Payment Terms

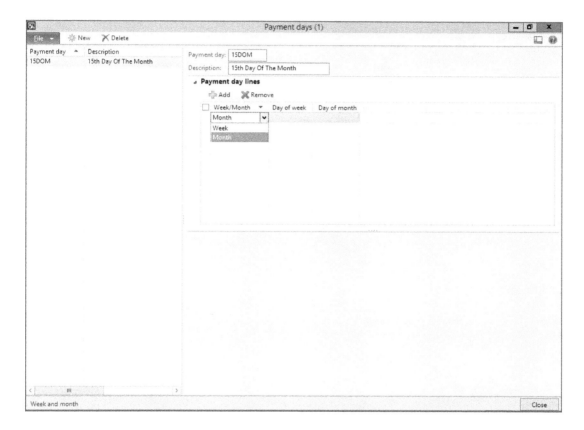

Then within the **Payment Day Lines** table, select the **Month** option from the **Week/Month** dropdown list.

Configuring Net Day Of Month Payment Terms

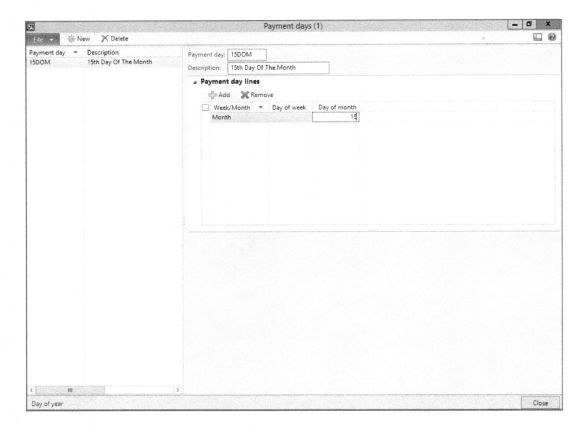

Then set the **Day Of Month** to the date that you want the payments due on, which in this case is **15**.

Configuring Net Day Of Month Payment Terms

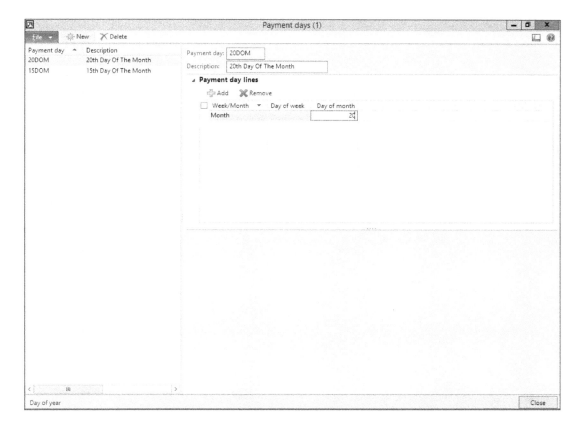

If you want to create variations of this then you can keep on adding new records.

When you are done, just click the **Close** button to exit from the form.

Configuring Net Day Of Month Payment Terms

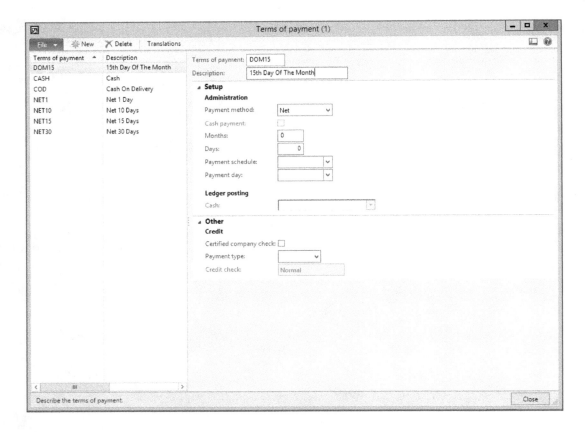

Now return to the **Terms Of Payment** maintenance form, and click on the **New** button to add a new record.

Set the **Terms Of Payment** to **DOM15**, and the **Description** to **15th Day Of The Month**.

Configuring Net Day Of Month Payment Terms

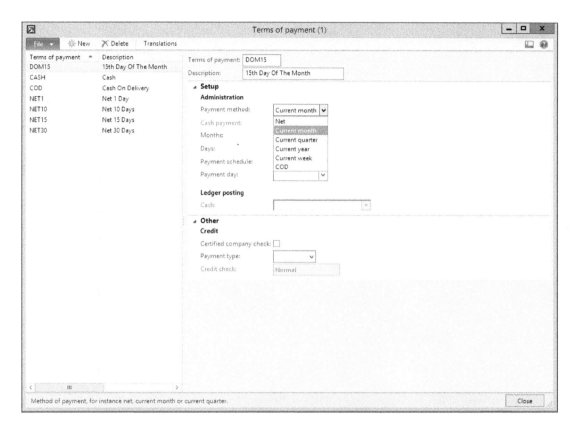

From the **Payment Method** dropdown, select the **Current Month** option.

Configuring Net Day Of Month Payment Terms

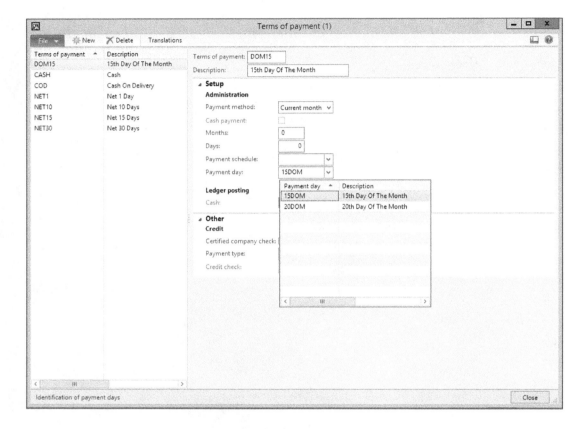

And then from the **Payment Day** dropdown field select the **15DOM** record that you just created.

Configuring Net Day Of Month Payment Terms

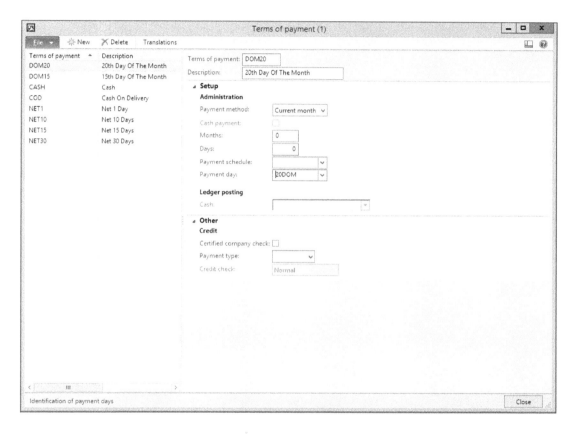

If you created any additional Payment Day records, then you can repeat the process to add additional **Terms Of Payment** for them.

Configuring Equal Monthly Scheduled Payment Terms

Payment terms don't have to be just a lump sum payment, you can also configure payment schedules with multiple payment dates. The first type of payment schedule that you may want to configure is a monthly payment for a set number of months.

Configuring Equal Monthly Scheduled Payment Terms

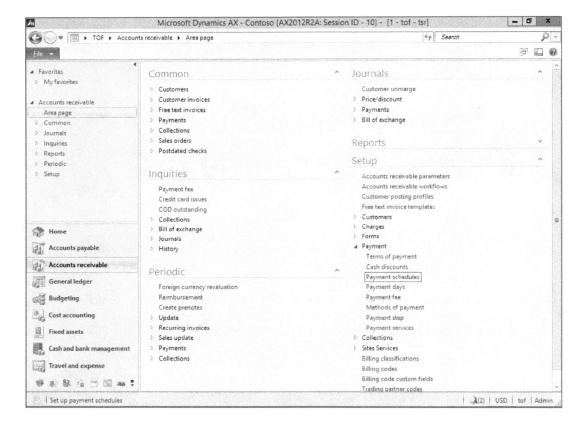

To do this, click on the **Payment Schedules** menu item within the **Payment** folder of the **Setup** group within the **Accounts Receivable** area page.

Configuring Equal Monthly Scheduled Payment Terms

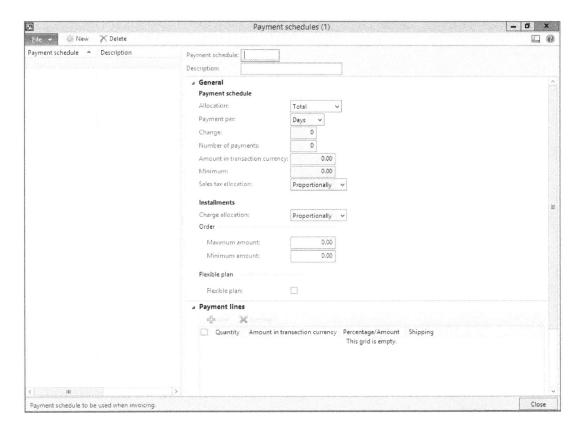

When the **Payment Schedules** maintenance form is displayed, click on the **New** button in the menu bar to create a new record.

Configuring Equal Monthly Scheduled Payment Terms

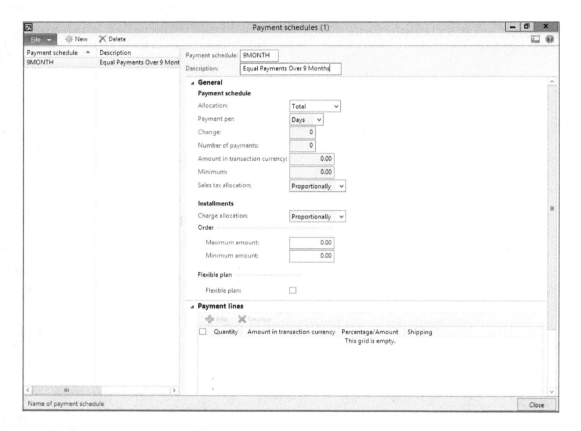

Then set the **Payment Schedule** code to **9MONTH** and the description to **Equal Payments Over 9 Months**.

Configuring Equal Monthly Scheduled Payment Terms

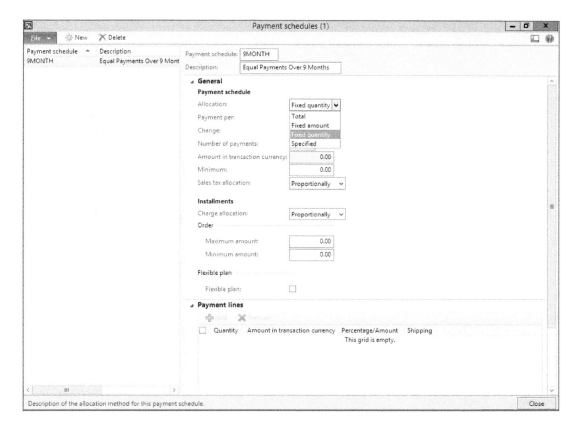

From the **Allocation** field drop down, select the **Fixed Quantity** option to tell the system that you want to have equal payments over a set number of intervals.

Configuring Equal Monthly Scheduled Payment Terms

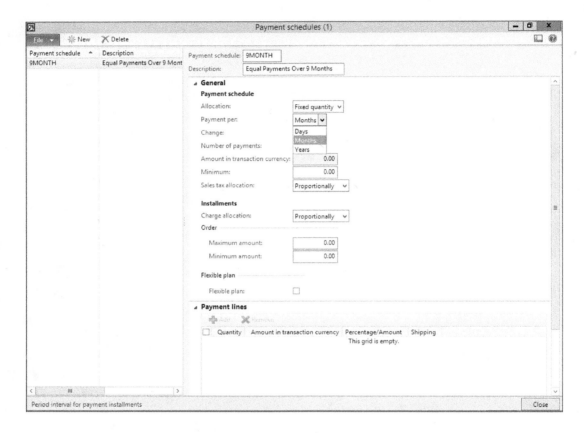

Then select the **Months** option from the **Payment Per** dropdown list.

Configuring Equal Monthly Scheduled Payment Terms

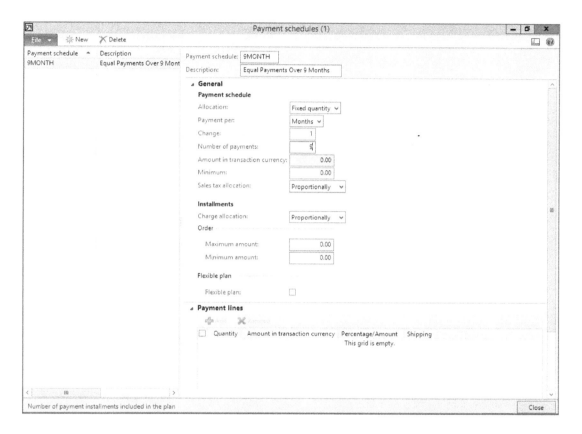

Then type in the **Number Of Payments** that you want to have within the schedule. In this case we chose **9**.

After you have done this you can add additional payment schedule variations, and when you are done, just click on the **Close** button to exit from the form.

Configuring Equal Monthly Scheduled Payment Terms

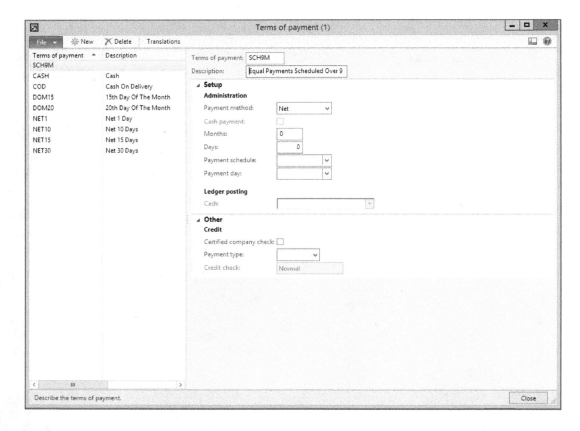

Now return to the **Terms Of Payments** maintenance form and click the **New** button in the menu bar to create a new record.

Then set the **Terms Of Payment** code to be **SCH6M** and the **Description** to **Equal Payments Scheduled over 9 Months**.

Configuring Equal Monthly Scheduled Payment Terms

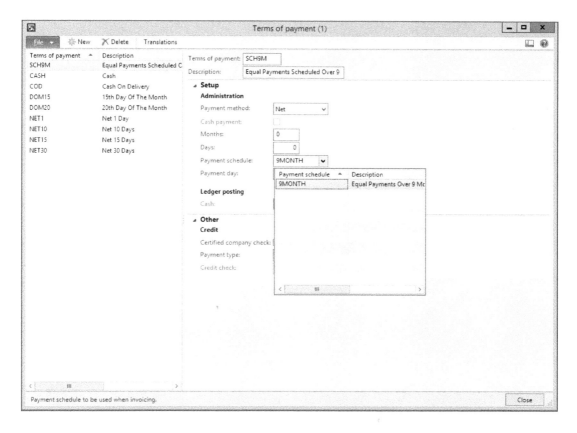

Set the **Payment Method** to be **Net** and then from the **Payment Schedule** field, select the new monthly schedule that you just created.

After you have done that you can click on the **Close** button and exit from the form.

Configuring Proportional Monthly Scheduled Payment Terms

Another variation of the monthly payment schedule that you can create within Dynamics AX is a proportional payment schedule with varying payment percentages by month. With this you could required lump sums up front, or have balloon payments structured at the end of the payments.

Configuring Proportional Monthly Scheduled Payment Terms

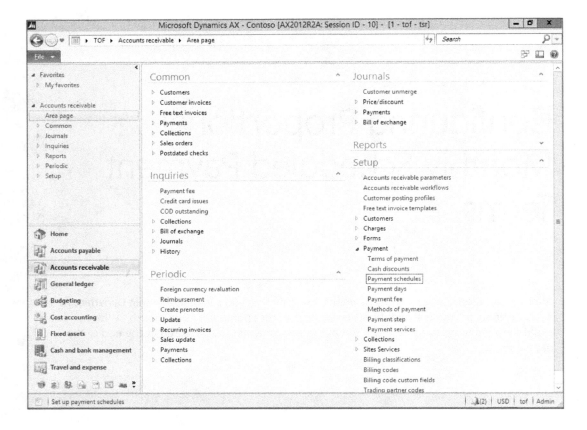

To do this, click on the **Payment Schedules** menu item within the **Payment** folder of the **Setup** group within the **Accounts Receivable** area page.

Configuring Proportional Monthly Scheduled Payment Terms

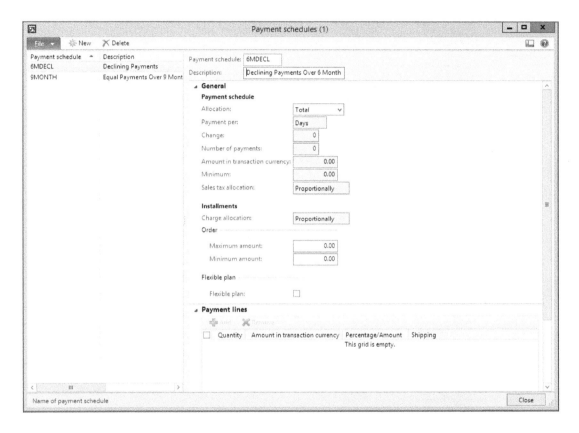

When the **Payment Schedules** maintenance form is displayed, click on the **New** button in the menu bar to create a new record.

Then set the **Payment Schedule** code to **6MDECL** and the description to **Declining Payments Over 6 Months**.

Configuring Proportional Monthly Scheduled Payment Terms

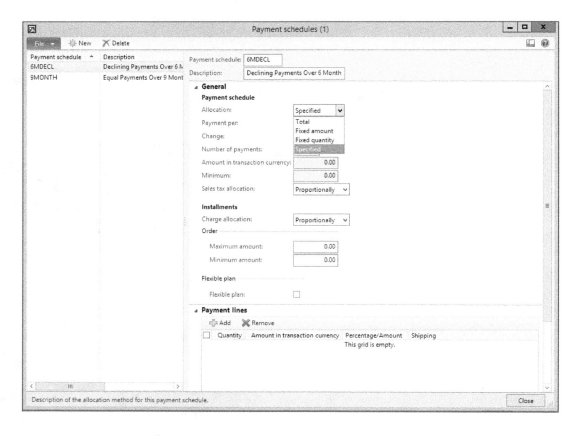

Then from the **Allocation** dropdown list select the **Specified** option.

Configuring Proportional Monthly Scheduled Payment Terms

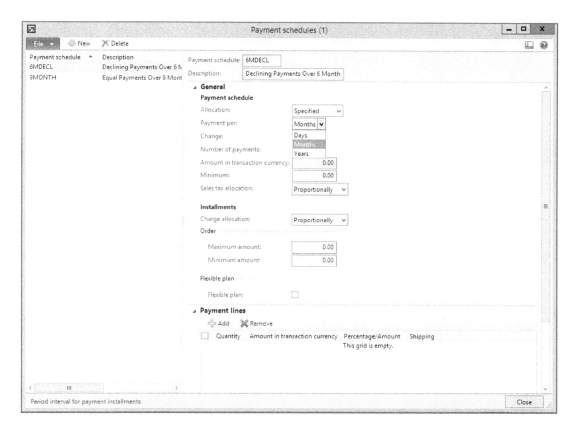

Set the **Payment Term** field to **Months** to identify that we are going to have monthly payments.

Configuring Proportional Monthly Scheduled Payment Terms

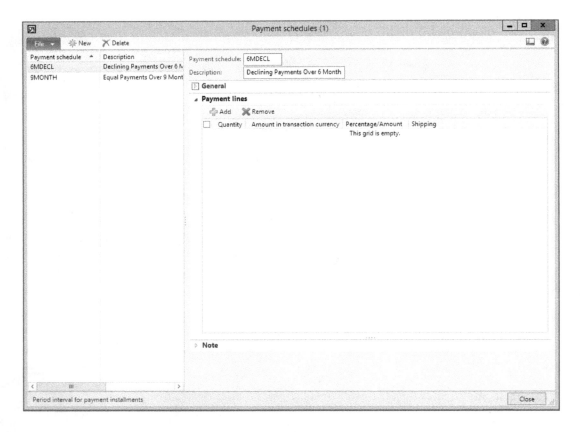

Now collapse the **General group** so that you can see the **Payment Lines** tab group.

Configuring Proportional Monthly Scheduled Payment Terms

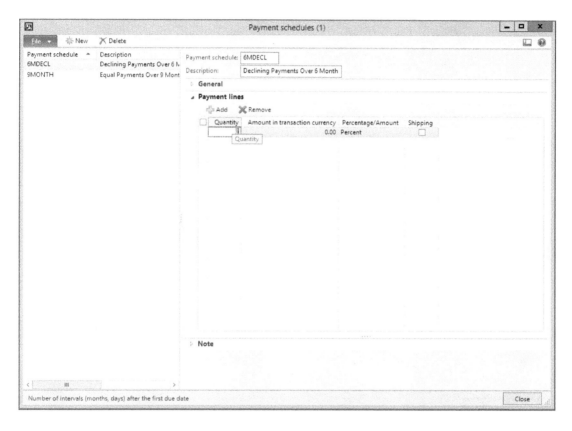

Click on the **Add** button in the **Payment Lines** table to create a new payment line record and set the **Quantity** to 1 to create a record for the first month.

Configuring Proportional Monthly Scheduled Payment Terms

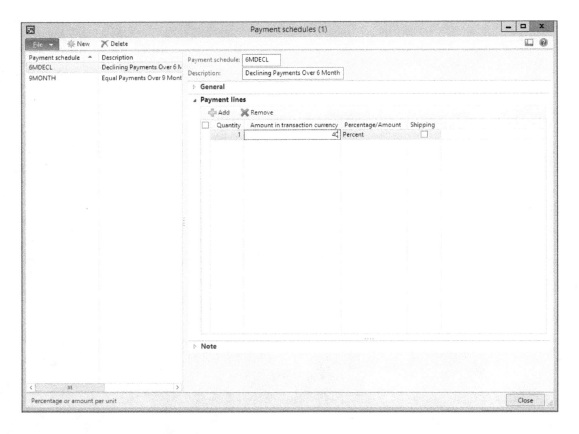

Then set the **Amount In Transaction Currency** field to be the percentage of payment that is due in that first month.

Configuring Proportional Monthly Scheduled Payment Terms

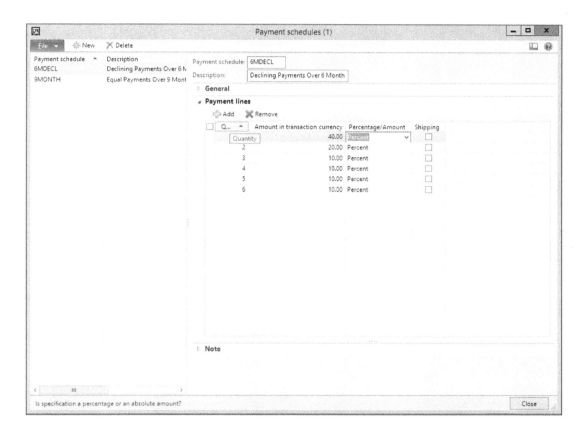

Repeat the process for all of the other months that you require payments along with the percentage amount. Make sure that they add up to 100% so that you are not giving away money.

When you are done, click on the **Close** button to exit from the form.

Configuring Proportional Monthly Scheduled Payment Terms

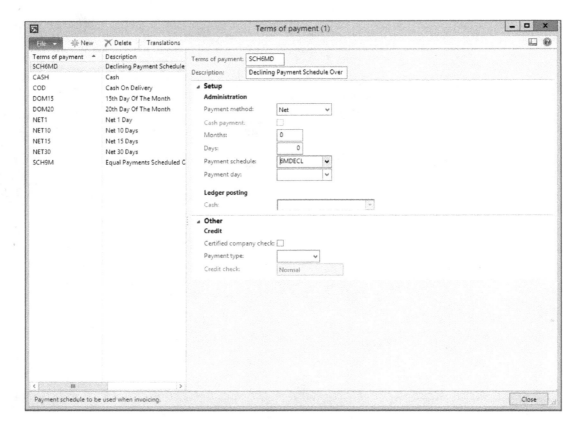

Now return to the **Terms Of Payments** maintenance form and click the **New** button in the menu bar to create a new record.

Then set the **Terms Of Payment** code to be **SCH6M** and the **Description** to **Equal Payments Scheduled over 9 Months**.

Set the **Payment Method** to be **Net** and then from the **Payment Schedule** field, select the new proportional monthly schedule that you just created.

After you have done that you can click on the **Close** button and exit from the form.

Configuring Cash Discount Codes

In addition to configuring the **Terms Of Payments** you may also want to configure **Cash Discount Codes** as incentives for early payment with discount percentages.

Configuring Cash Discount Codes

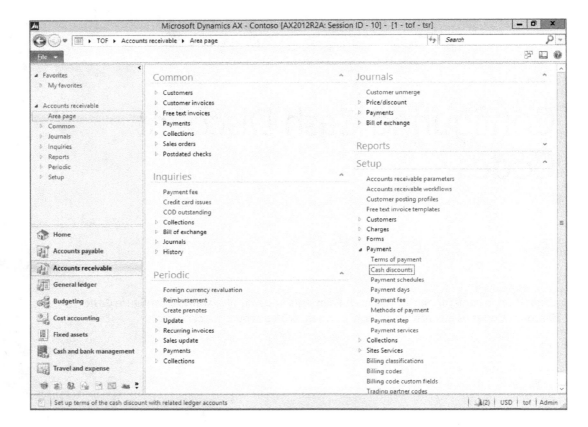

To do this, click on the **Cash Discounts** menu item within the **Payments** folder of the **Setup** group of the **Accounts Receivable** area page.

Configuring Cash Discount Codes

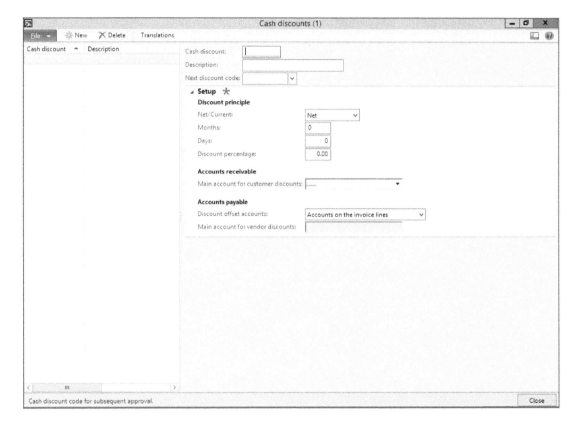

When the **Cash Discounts** maintenance form is displayed, click on the **New** button in the menu bar to create a new record.

Configuring Cash Discount Codes

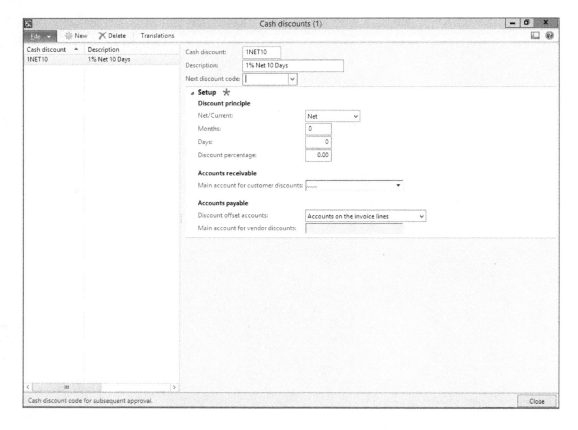

Then set the **Cash Discount** code to **1NET10** and the **Description** to **1% Net 10** which seems like a reasonable discount to give for early payment.

Configuring Cash Discount Codes

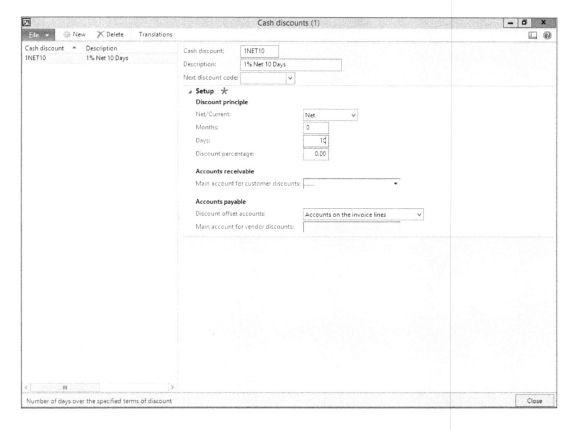

Set the **Days** field to be the number of days that you want to encourage the customer to pay in – in our case **10**.

Configuring Cash Discount Codes

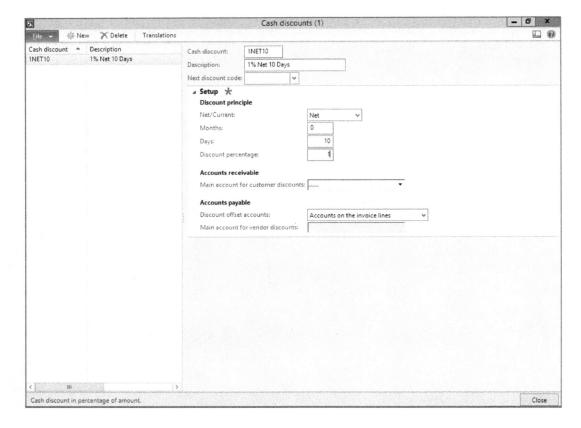

And then in the **Discount Percentage** field set the discount percentage that you want to give the customer. We set ours to **1**.

Configuring Cash Discount Codes

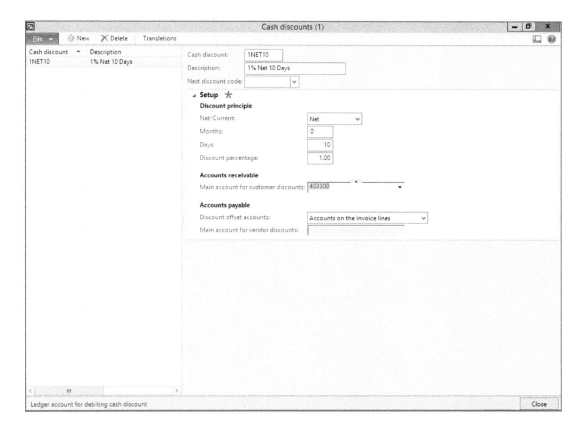

Then assign a **Main Account For Customer Discounts** to identify where the discount is going to be posted to.

Configuring Cash Discount Codes

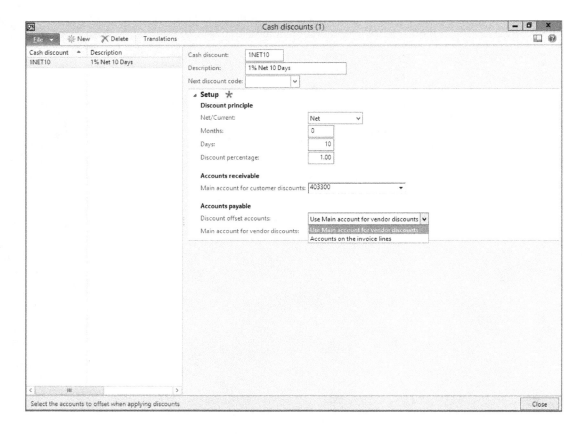

These Cash Discounts codes are also used for the Accounts Payable discounts – no point in reinventing the wheel. So while we are here we will also configure the AP settings for the discounts so that we don't need to set them up later on. To do this, select the **Use Main Account For Vendor Discounts** option from the **Discount Offset Accounts** field.

Configuring Cash Discount Codes

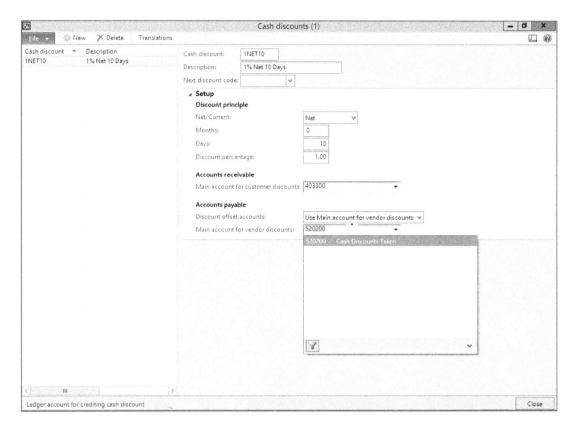

And then select the **Main Account For Vendor Discounts** that you want to post the Vendor Discounts to.

Configuring Cash Discount Codes

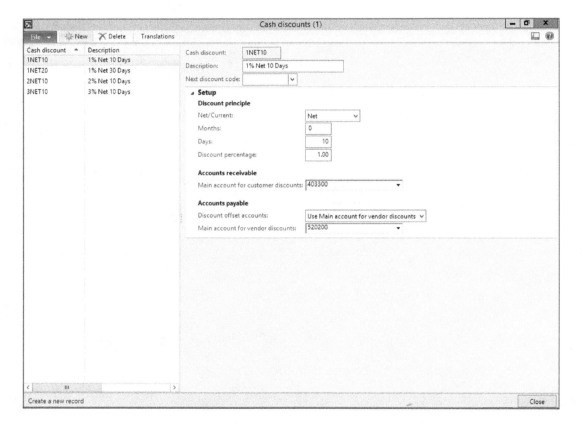

You can repeat this process for any other combinations and variations of the discount terms that you want to offer to your customers, and when you a done, just click on the **Close** button to exit from the form.

Configuring Cash Payment Methods

Now we need to configure a few different methods for receiving cash. The first one that we will configure is a Cash payment method.

Configuring Cash Payment Methods

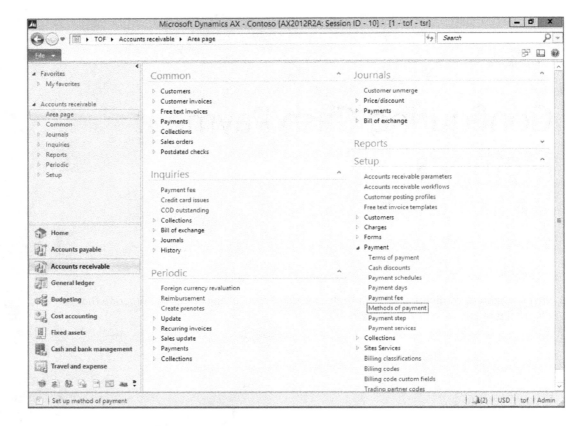

To do this, click on the **Methods Of Payment** menu item within the **Payment** folder of the **Setup** group of the **Accounts Receivable** area page.

Configuring Cash Payment Methods

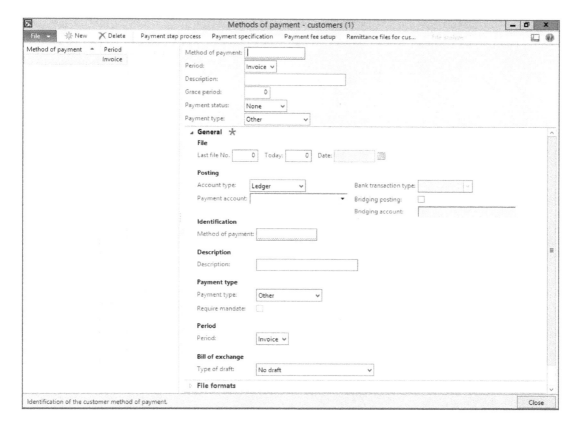

When the **Methods Of Payment** maintenance form is displayed, click on the **New** button within the menu bar to create a new record.

Configuring Cash Payment Methods

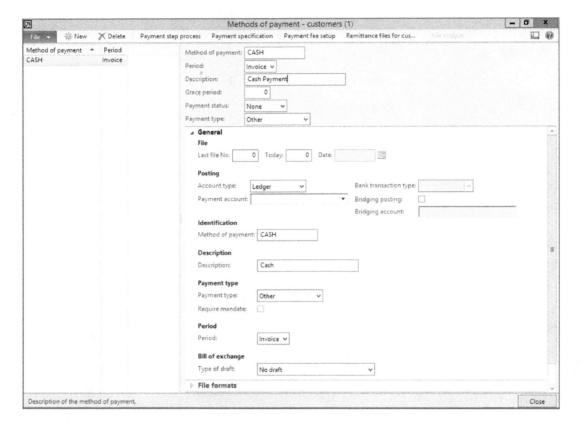

Set the **Method Of Payment** code to **CASH** and set the **Description** to be **Cash Payment**.

Configuring Cash Payment Methods

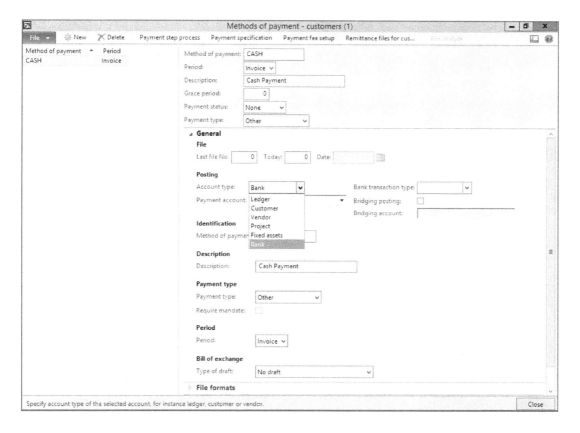

From within the **General** tab, set the **Account Type** to **Bank**.

Configuring Cash Payment Methods

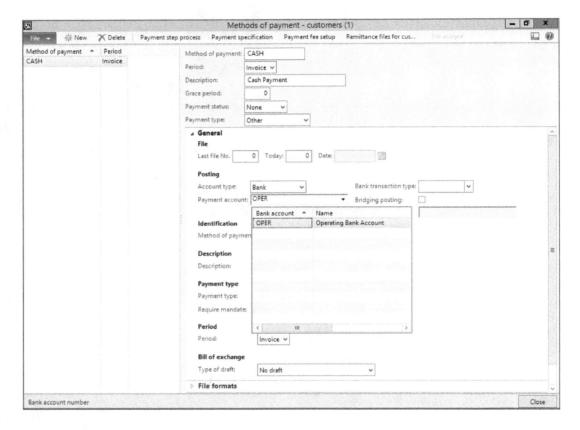

And then select the bank that you want to post the cash to from the **Payment Account** dropdown list.

Configuring Cash Payment Methods

To make your life a little easier later on when you start looking at performing Bank Reconciliations, also set the **Bank Transaction Type** to be the correct code – for us it's **01**.

Configuring Cash Payment Methods

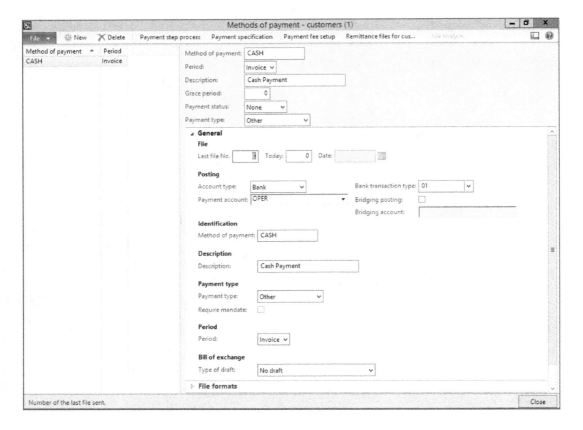

Once you have done that you can click on the **Close** button and exit the form.

Configuring Check Payment Methods

Another common payment method that you may want to accept are checks.

Configuring Check Payment Methods

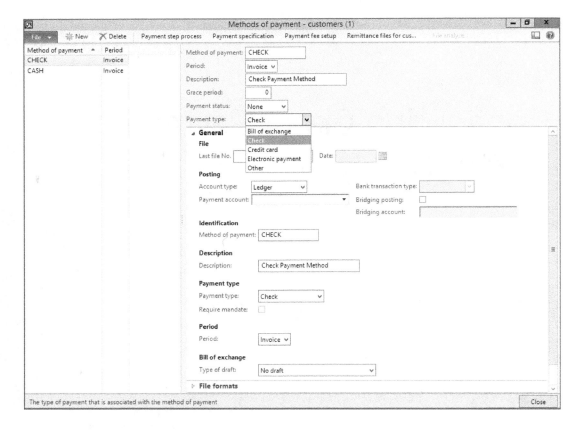

To add a check payment type, open up the **Methods Of Payment** maintenance form and click on the **New** button within the menu bar to create a new record.

Then set the **Method Of Payment** to **CHECK** and the **Description** to **Check Payment Method**.

From the **Payment Type** dropdown field, select the **Check** option.

Configuring Check Payment Methods

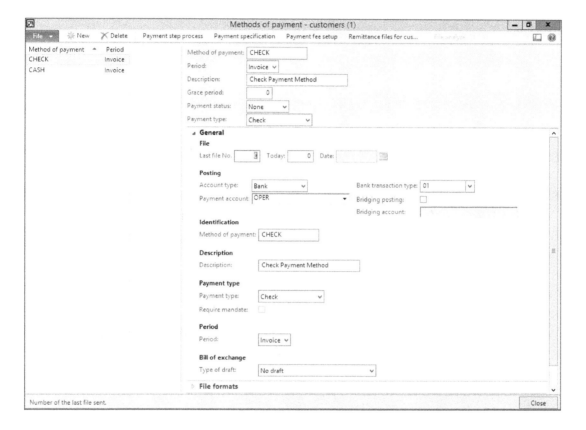

Then set the **Account Type** to be **Bank**, select the bank that you want to deposit the checks into from the **Payment Account** dropdown list and then set the **Bank Transaction Type** to **01.**

Configuring Electronic Payment Methods

If you accept payments electronically then you will probably want to configure an Electronic Payment Method.

Configuring Electronic Payment Methods

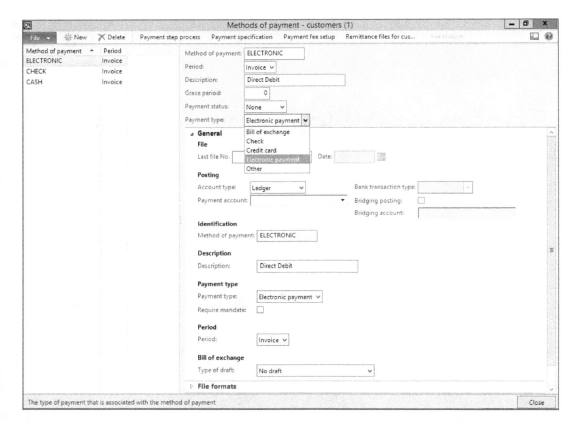

To add a check payment type, open up the **Methods Of Payment** maintenance form and click on the **New** button within the menu bar to create a new record.

Then set the **Method Of Payment** to **ELECTRONIC** and the **Description** to **Direct Debit**.

From the **Payment Type** dropdown field, select the **Electronic Payment** option.

Configuring Electronic Payment Methods

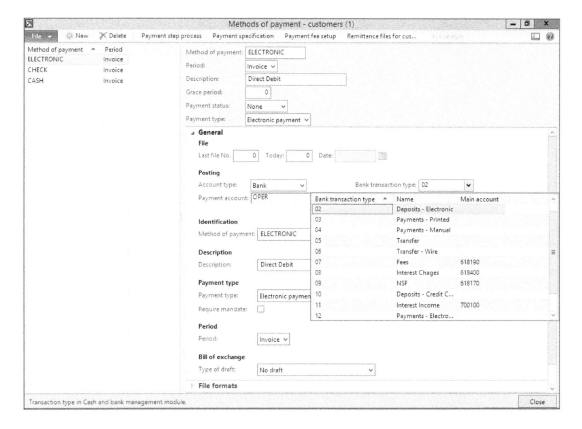

Then set the **Account Type** to be **Bank**, and select the bank that you want to deposit the checks into from the **Payment Account** dropdown list.

For this transaction, set the **Bank Transaction Type** to **02** for the electronic deposit transaction type.

Configuring Postdated Check Payment Methods

If you accept postdated checks then there is a slightly different configuration that you want to use, rather than the standard check Payment Method.

Configuring Postdated Check Payment Methods

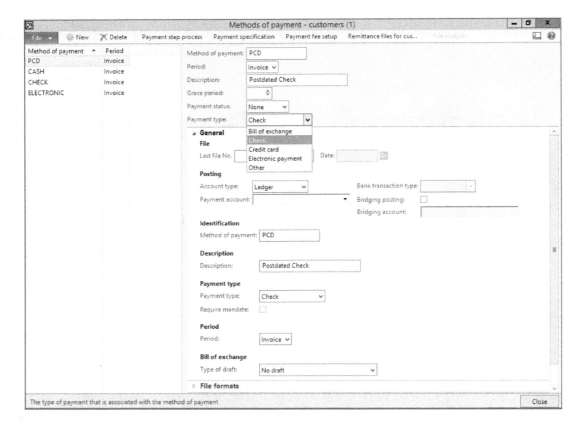

To add a check payment type, open up the **Methods Of Payment** maintenance form and click on the **New** button within the menu bar to create a new record.

Then set the **Method Of Payment** to **PDC** and the **Description** to **Postdated Check**.

From the **Payment Type** dropdown field, select the **Check** option.

Configuring Postdated Check Payment Methods

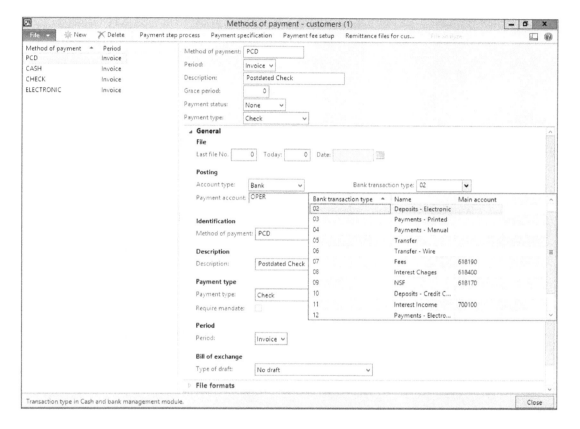

Then set the **Account Type** to be **Bank**, and select the bank that you want to deposit the checks into from the **Payment Account** dropdown list.

For this transaction, set the **Bank Transaction Type** to **02** for the electronic deposit transaction type.

Configuring Postdated Check Payment Methods

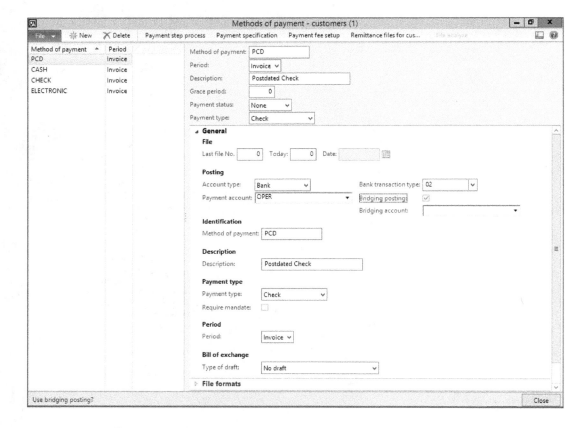

Then check the **Bridging Posting** flag.

Configuring Postdated Check Payment Methods

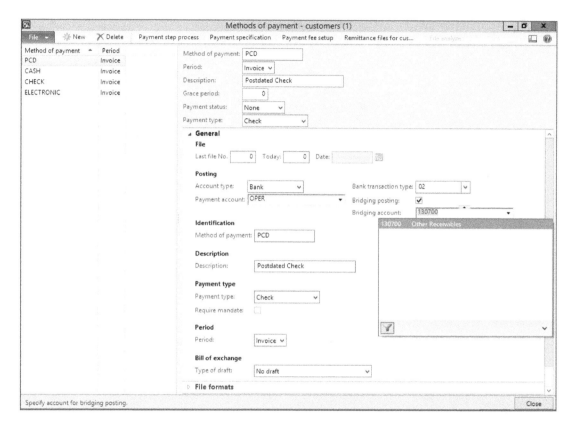

This will allow you to select a main account from the **Bridging Account** dropdown to post the postdated check amounts to.

Configuring Postdated Check Payment Methods

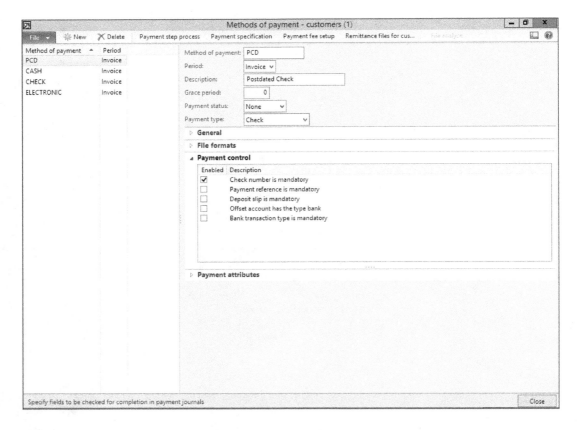

And then open up the **Payment Control** tab group and check the **Check Number Is Mandatory** option to ensure that the check number is tracked within the system.

After you have done that you can click on the **Close** button to exit from the form.

Configuring Refund Payment Methods

Although you probably don't want to give refunds, there may be a need for them within the system, so we need to configure one last Payment Method to manage this.

Configuring Refund Payment Methods

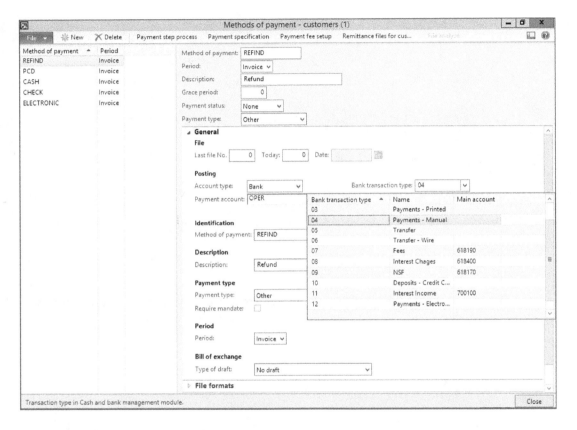

To add a check payment type, open up the **Methods Of Payment** maintenance form and click on the **New** button within the menu bar to create a new record.

Then set the **Method Of Payment** to **REFUND** and the **Description** to **Refund**.

From the **Payment Type** dropdown field, select the **Other** option.

Then set the **Account Type** to be **Bank**, and select the bank that you want to pay the refund from the **Payment Account** dropdown list.

For this transaction, set the **Bank Transaction Type** to **04** for the manual payment transaction type.

After you have done that you can click on the **Close** button to exit from the form.

Configuring Accounts Receivable Parameters

Now that we have all of the main codes and controls configured for the Accounts Receivable area within Dynamics AX, we will tie up the last loose ends by tweaking a couple of the options within the **Accounts Receivable Parameters.**

Configuring Accounts Receivable Parameters

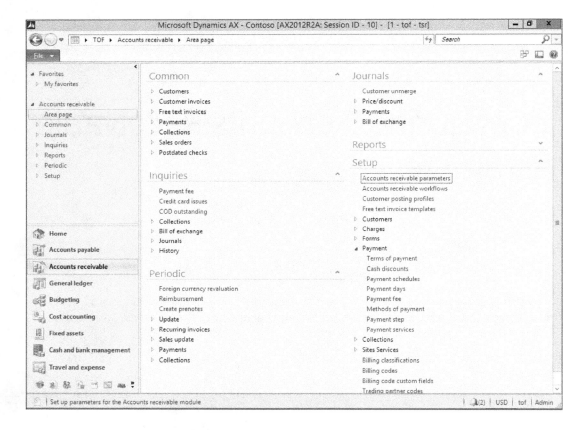

To do this, click on the **Accounts Receivable Parameters** menu item within the **Setup** group of the **Accounts Receivable** area page.

Configuring Accounts Receivable Parameters

When the **Accounts Receivable Parameters** form is displayed, click on the **General** group on the left had side to view the **General** parameters.

Configuring Accounts Receivable Parameters

The first thing that we will do is change the **Default Order Type** from **Journal** to **Sales Order** so that we will be able to ship our orders after entering them.

Configuring Accounts Receivable Parameters

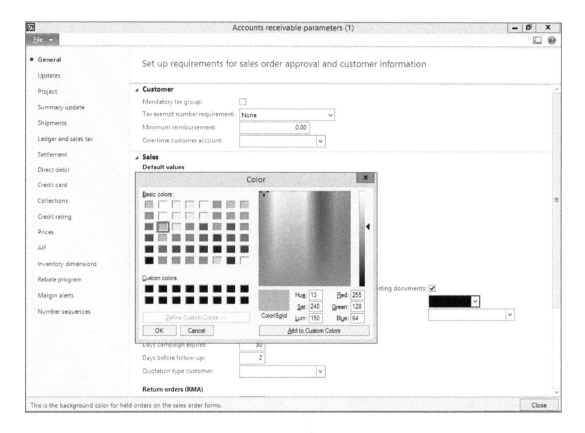

Then click on the color chooser for the **Order Hold For Order Status** field. When the color chooser is displayed, you can select a less depressing color that will be used to highlight that orders are on hold. Black is too dreary.

Configuring Accounts Receivable Parameters

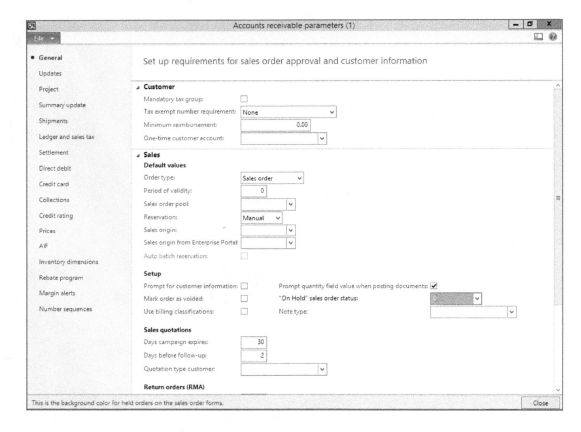

After you have done that your general configuration is done.

Configuring Accounts Receivable Parameters

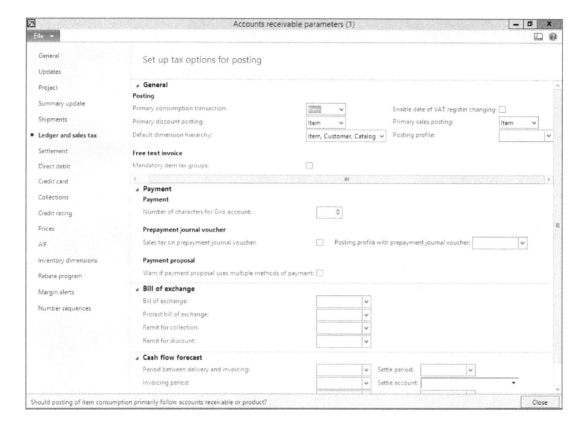

Next, switch to the **Ledger And Sales Tax** options page.

Configuring Accounts Receivable Parameters

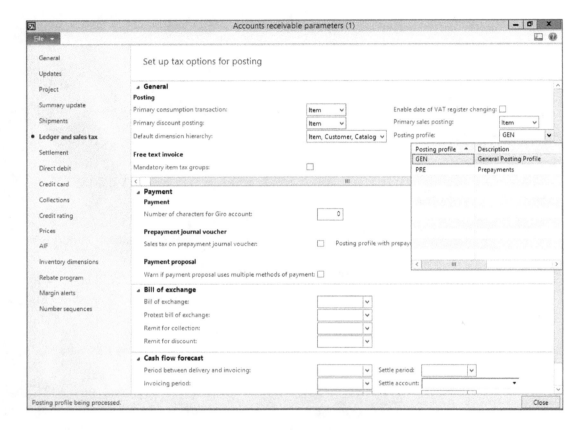

From within the **General** tab group, click on the **Posting Profile** dropdown and select the **GEN** posting profile that you set up earlier.

Configuring Accounts Receivable Parameters

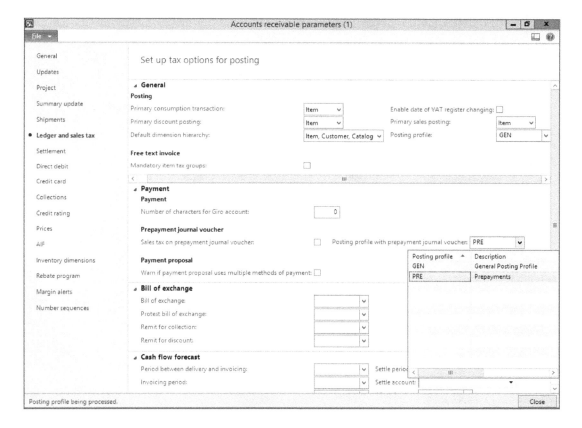

Then from within the **Payment** tab group, select the **PRE** posting profile that you configured earlier from the dropdown list for the **Posting Profile With Prepayment Journal Voucher** field.

Configuring Accounts Receivable Parameters

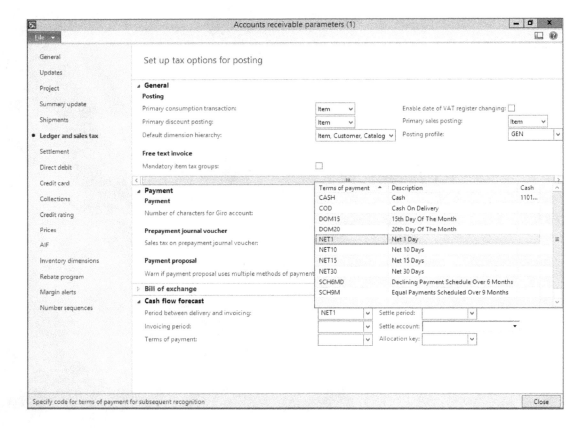

Within the **Cash Flow Forecast** tab group we should configure a few more defaults. First select a **Term Of Payment** for the **Period Between Delivery and Invoicing** for the default payment terms.

Configuring Accounts Receivable Parameters

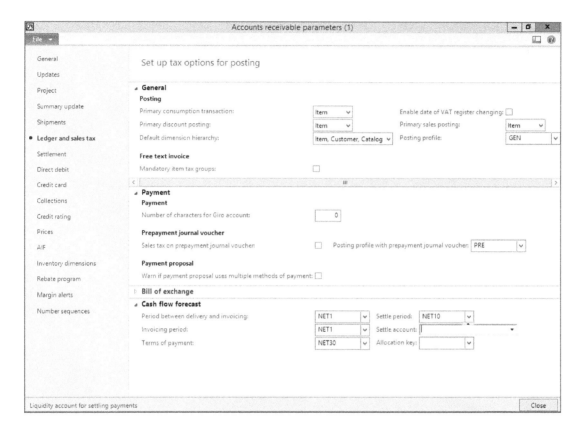

Also do the same for the **Invoicing Period**, the **Terms Of Payment** and the **Settle Period**.

Configuring Accounts Receivable Parameters

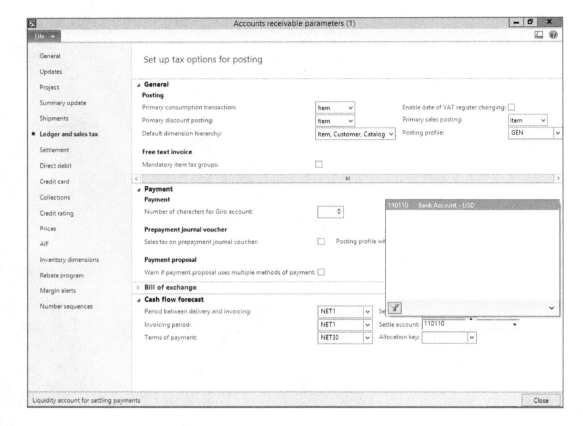

Then select the account that you want to use as the **Settle Account**. In this example we just used the operating bank account.

Configuring Accounts Receivable Parameters

Configuring Accounts Receivable Parameters

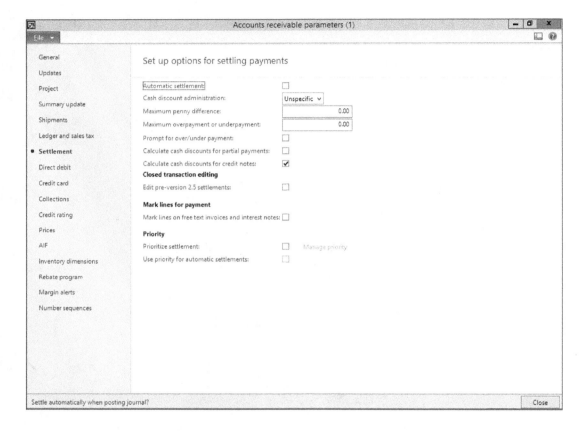

Now switch to the **Settlement** options page.

Configuring Accounts Receivable Parameters

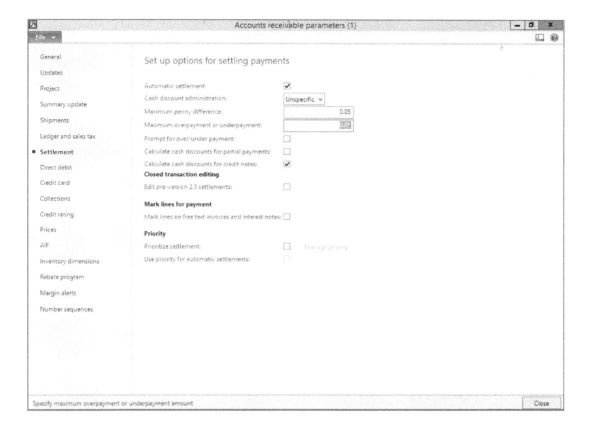

Check the **Automatic Settlement** and also set the **Maximum Penny Difference** and the **Maximum Overpayment And Underpayment** tolerances. We will accept 5 cents either way, although you could be stricter or a little more flexible.

After you have done this you can click on the **Close** button to exit from the form.

CONFIGURING CUSTOMER ACCOUNTS

Once you have all the base configuration done within the Accounts Receivable area, you can start getting to the meat and potatoes of the module, which is the configuration of the **Customer Accounts**. This may seem like a daunting task if you have a large customer base, but if you use the import tools, and features like the Excel Add-In for tidying up your data, then this isn't very hard, and regardless of if you have 100, or 10,000 customers can be a breeze to load.

Changing the Customer Numbering Sequence

Before we start though we will make one quick tweak to the system to allow us to use manual numbering for the customer accounts. You don't have to do this and can have Dynamics AX assign customer numbers for you automatically, but if you are like most companies you may want to add some of your own intelligence to the numbering format.

Changing the Customer Numbering Sequence

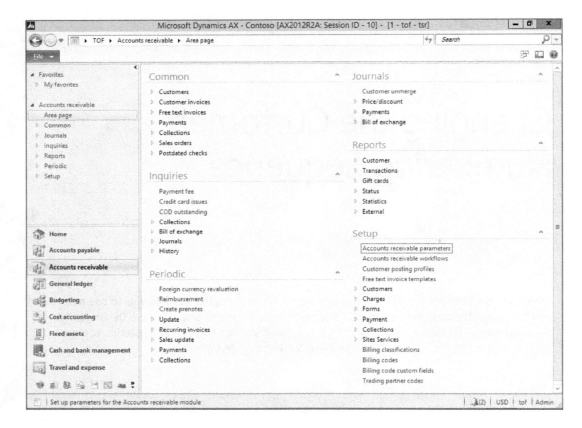

To do this, click on the **Accounts Receivable Parameters** menu item within the **Setup** group of the **Accounts Receivable** area page.

Changing the Customer Numbering Sequence

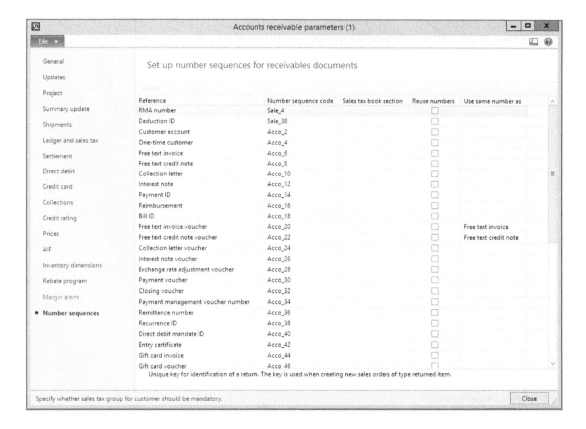

When the **Accounts Receivable Parameters** form is displayed, switch to the **Number Sequences** page.

Changing the Customer Numbering Sequence

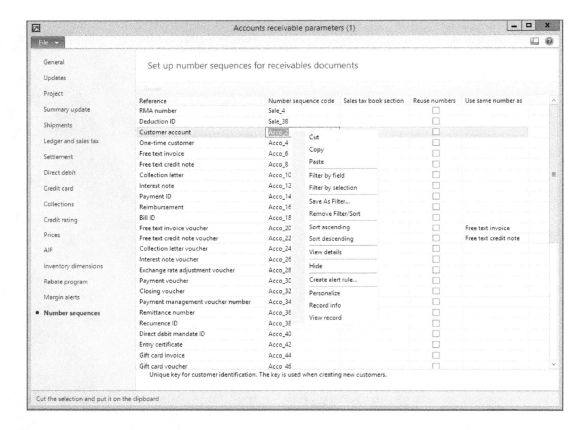

Then right-mouse-click on the number sequence for the **Customer Account** and select the **View Details** option.

Changing the Customer Numbering Sequence

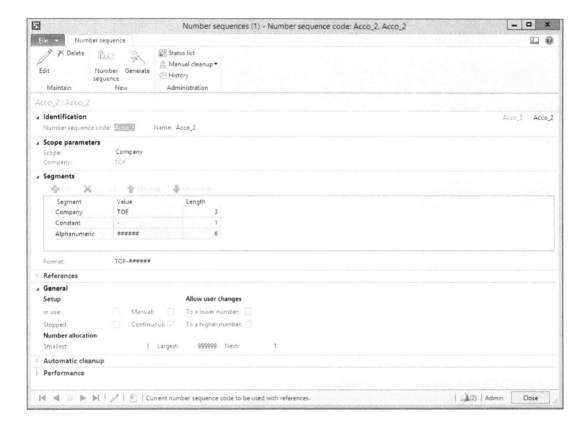

This will take you to the default number sequence for the Customer Number.

Changing the Customer Numbering Sequence

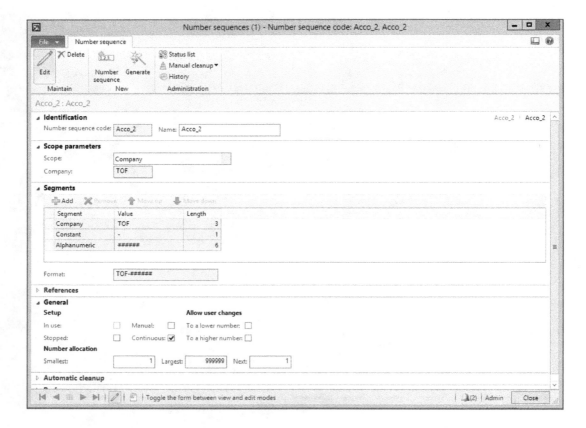

To make changes, click on the **Edit** button within the **Maintain** group of the **Number Sequence** ribbon bar.

Changing the Customer Numbering Sequence

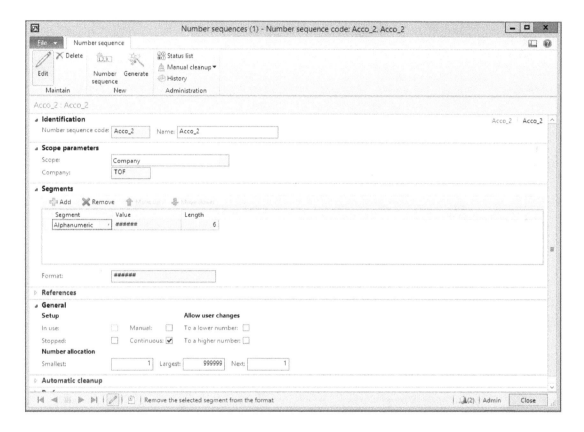

Click on the **Company** segment and click on the **Remove** button to remove the segment from the number sequence.

Do the same for the **Constant** so that you just have a simple customer number.

Changing the Customer Numbering Sequence

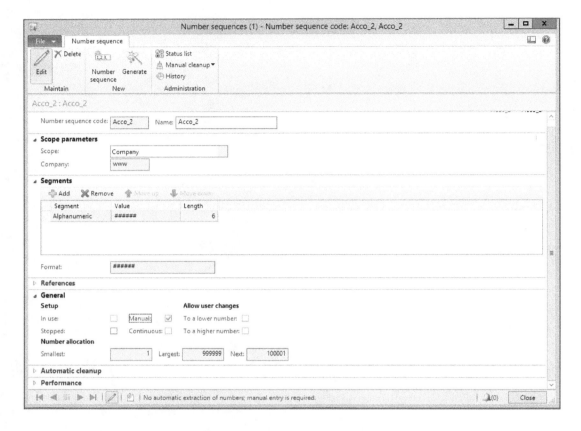

Then within the **General** tab group click on the **Manual** flag so that you will be able to assign customer numbers yourself.

After you have done this, click on the **Close** button to exit from the form, and then exit from the **Accounts Receivable Parameters** form by clicking on the **Close** button there as well.

Configuring Customer Groups

To save time and setup we will also configure the **Customer Groups** before we start adding customer accounts. These are a great way to segregate the customers, and also a great way to default in payment terms and tax groups.

Configuring Customer Groups

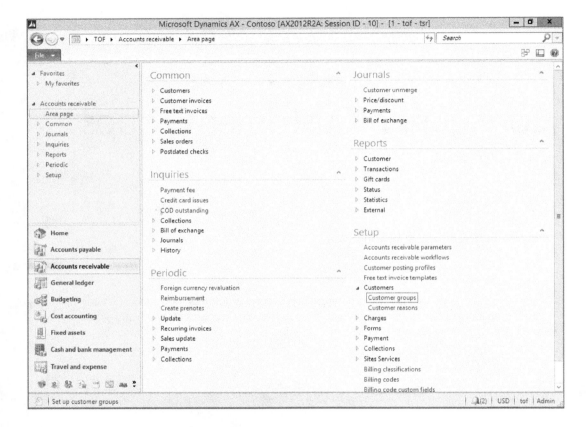

To do this, click on the **Customer Groups** menu item within the **Customers** folder of the **Setup** group within the **Accounts Receivable** area page.

Configuring Customer Groups

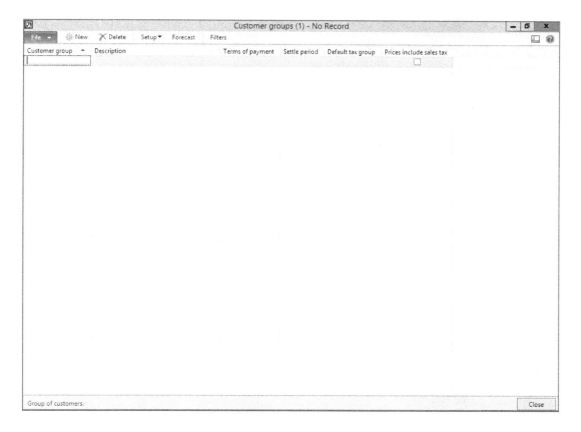

When the **Customer Groups** maintenance form is displayed, click on the **New** button to add a new record.

Configuring Customer Groups

Next assign your record a **Customer Group** code, and also a **Description**.

Configuring Customer Groups

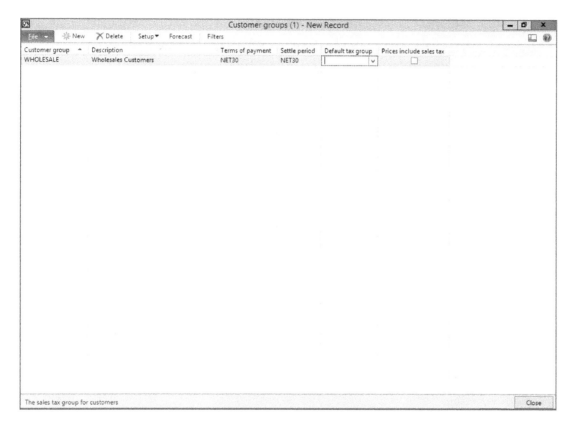

Then select the default **Terms Of Payment** and **Settle Period** that will be assigned to the customers that get assigned to the group.

Configuring Customer Groups

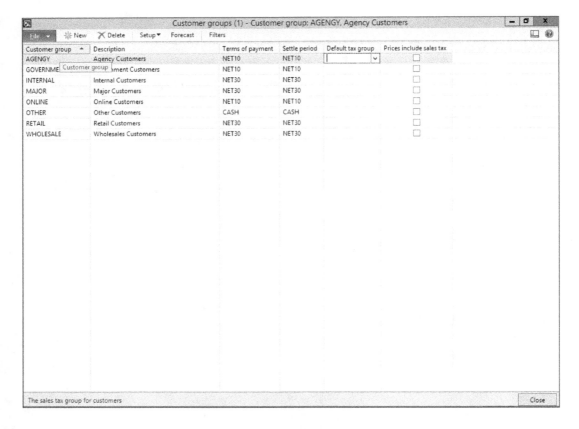

You can repeat this process for all of the other different types of customers that you will be tracking within the system.

When you are done, then just click the **Close** button to exit from the form.

Creating a New Customer Account

If you only have a select number of customers that you sell to then the quickest way to load them into the system is just by adding them one by one.

Creating a New Customer Account

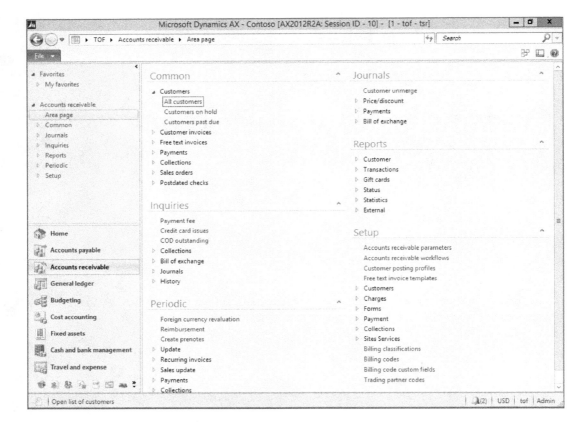

To add a new customer, just click on the **All Customers** menu item within the **Customers** folder of the **Common** group within the **Accounts Receivable** area page.

Creating a New Customer Account

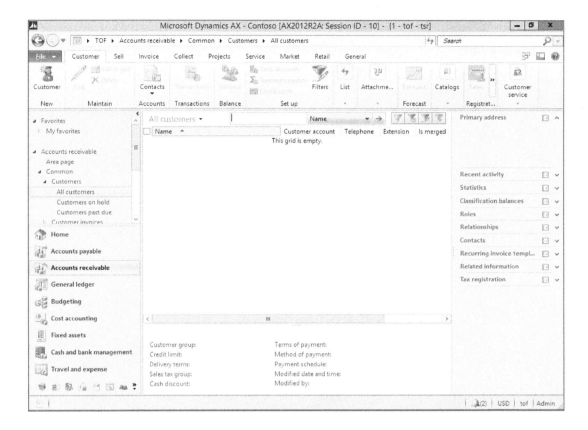

When the **Customers** list page is displayed, click on the **Customer** button within the **New** group of the **Customer** ribbon bar.

Creating a New Customer Account

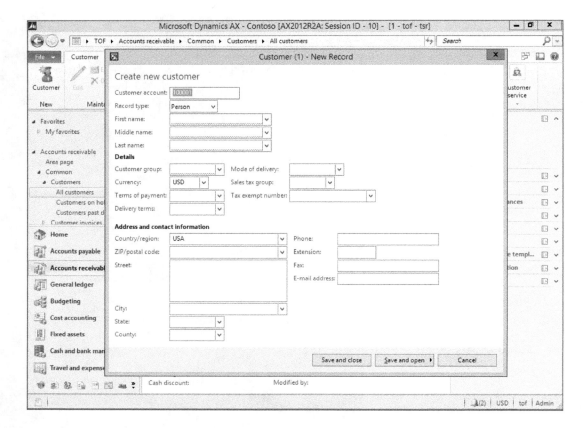

This will open up a Customer quick add dialog box. If you have manual numbering enabled then you can enter in a new **Customer Account**.

Creating a New Customer Account

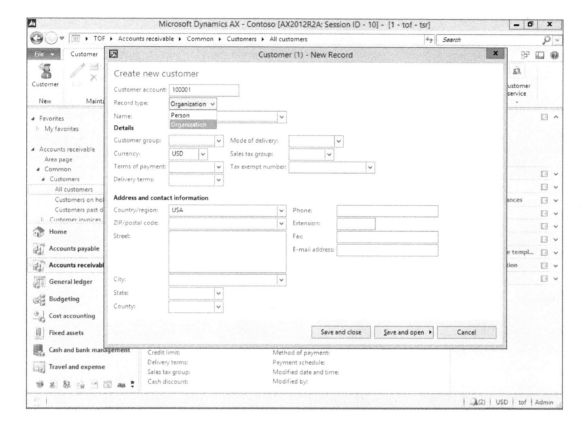

Customers are also configured either as a Person, or an Organization, each with their own specific naming format. If you want to change the **Record Type** from Person to Organization then just select it from the dropdown box.

Creating a New Customer Account

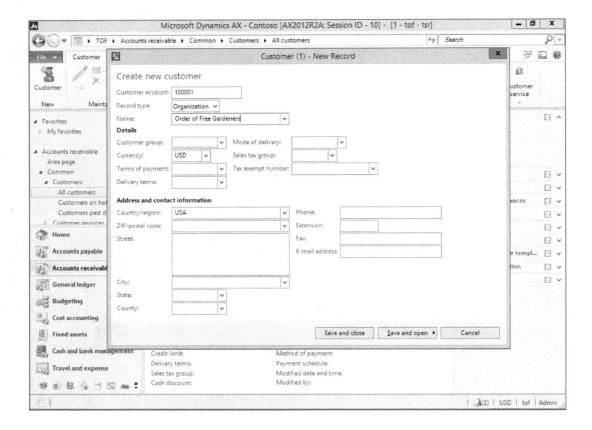

Now you can type in the **Name** for the organization.

Creating a New Customer Account

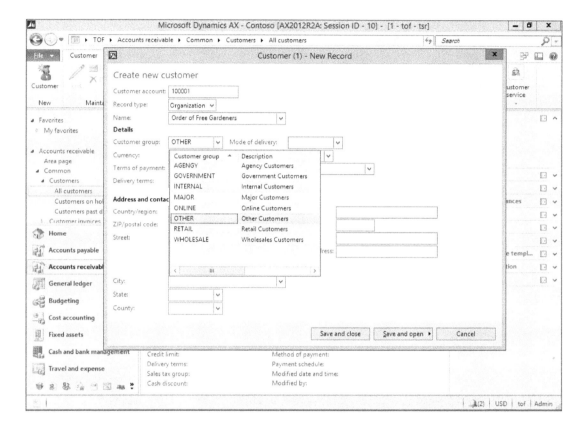

Next you want to assign the customer to a **Customer Group** by selecting it from the list of **Customer Groups** that you configured in the previous step.

Creating a New Customer Account

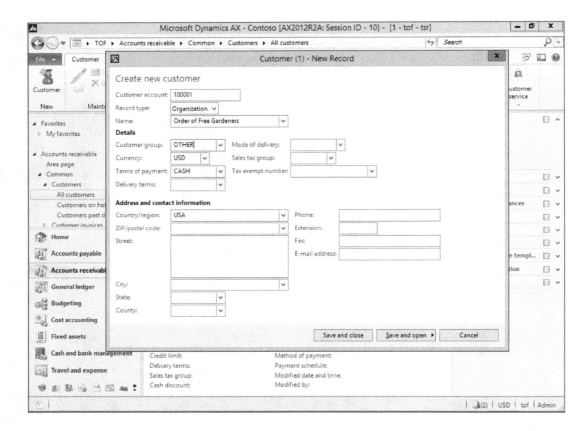

This will default in the Terms of Payment for you that you can override on a case by case basis if you like.

Creating a New Customer Account

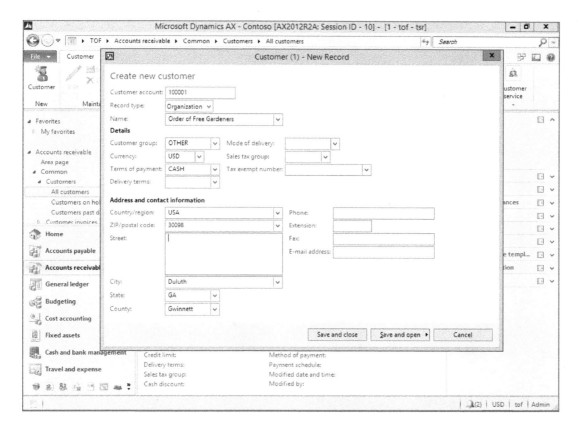

Now type in the **Zip/Postal Code** for the customer. Notice that it will pre-populate the **City**, **State**, and **County** if you have the regional data configured.

Creating a New Customer Account

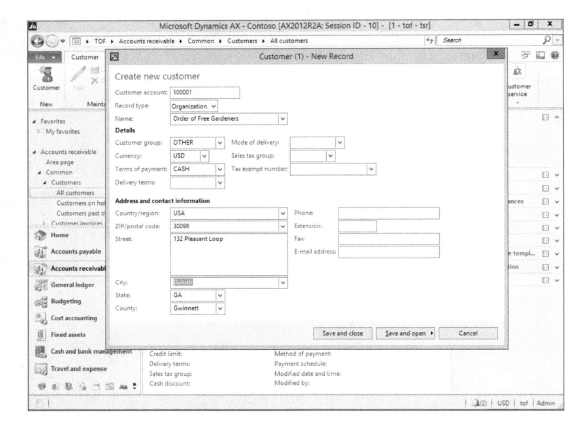

And then type in the **Street** address for the customer.

Creating a New Customer Account

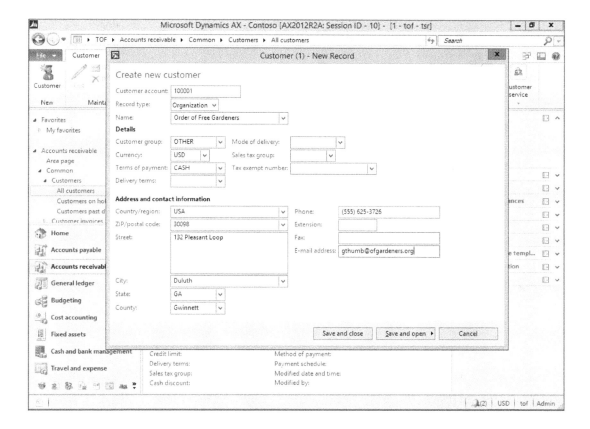

You can add additional information like the **Phone Number** and **Email Address** if you like.

Creating a New Customer Account

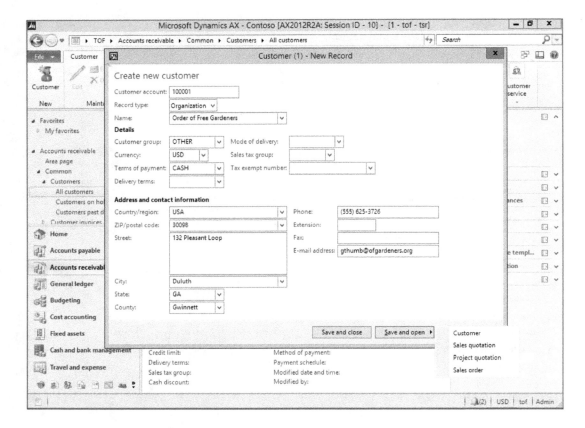

Now click on the **Save And Open** button and select the **Customer** option to go directly to the newly created customer account.

Creating a New Customer Account

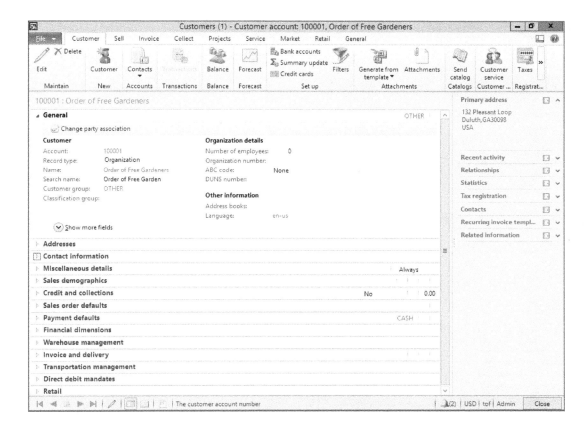

This will open up the **Customers** detail page for your new customer.

Creating a New Customer Account

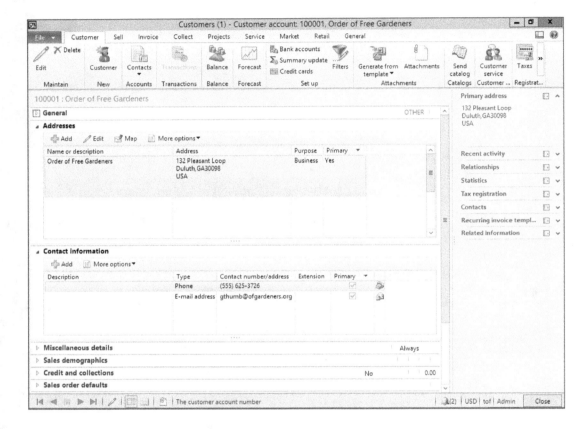

If you expand out the **Address** and **Contact Information** tab groups, then you will also see that the contact details have been populated as well.

Creating a New Customer Account

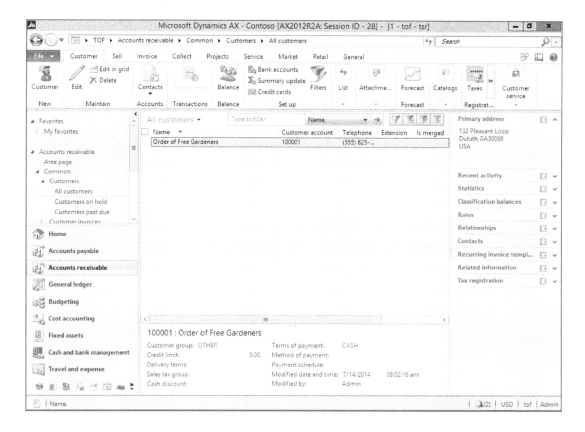

If you exit out of the **Customer** form by clicking on the **Close** button and refresh the **All Customers** list page you will see your new customer is now listed there.

Importing Customers Using The Data Import Export Framework

If you have more than a handful of customers though you may not want to have all of your customers entered by hand and you will probably want to import them. The easiest way to do that by far is the **Data Import Export Framework** and is super easy to configure without even requiring help from a developer or the IT department.

Importing Customers Using The Data Import Export Framework

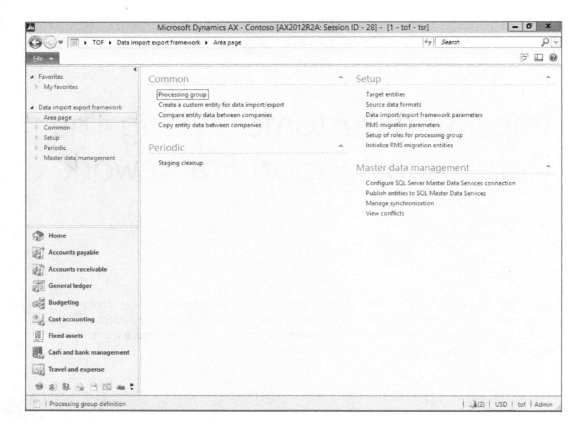

To do this, click on the **Processing Group** menu item within the **Common** group of the **Data Import Export Framework** area page.

Importing Customers Using The Data Import Export Framework

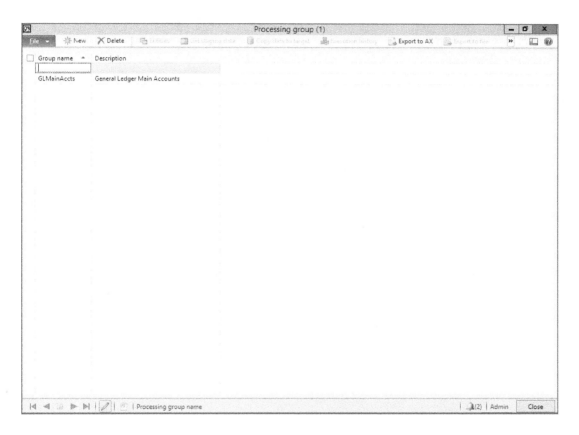

When the **Processing Groups** maintenance form is displayed, click on the **New** button within the menu bar to create a new record.

Importing Customers Using The Data Import Export Framework

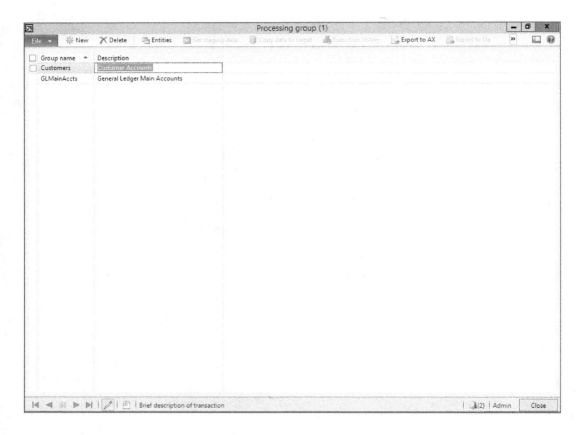

Set the **Group Name** to be **Customers** and the **Description** to be **Customer Accounts**.

Save the record (**CTRL+S**) and the **Entities** menu item will become enabled and you will be able to click on it.

Importing Customers Using The Data Import Export Framework

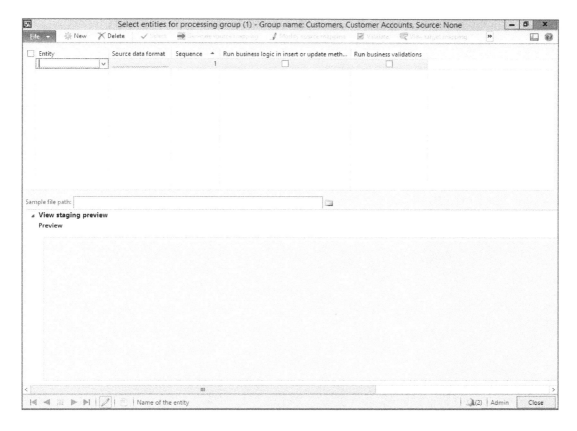

When the **Entities** maintenance form is displayed, click on the **New** button within the menu bar to create a new record.

Importing Customers Using The Data Import Export Framework

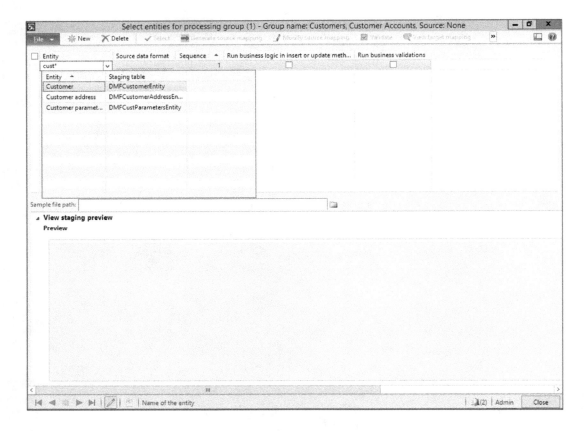

From the **Entity** field dropdown list, select the **Customer** entity.

Importing Customers Using The Data Import Export Framework

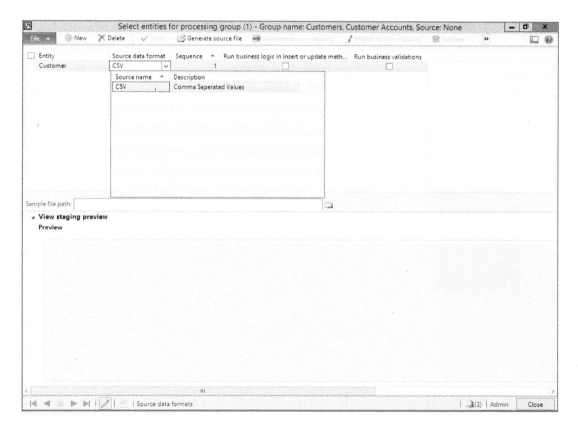

Then select the **CSV Source Data Format** that you used earlier on to import in the **GL Accounts**.

Now click on the **Generate Source File** button within the menu bar.

Importing Customers Using The Data Import Export Framework

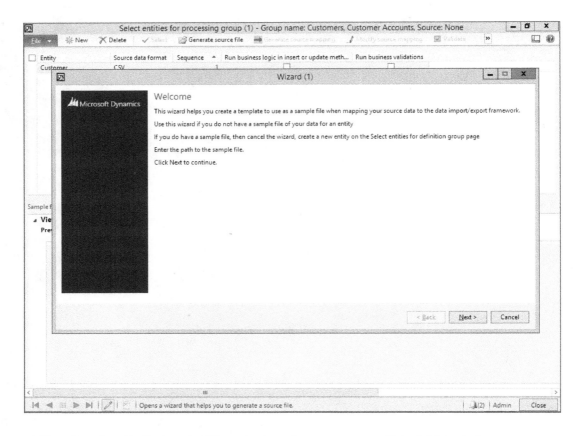

When the wizard is displayed, click on the **Next** button to move off the initial splash page.

Importing Customers Using The Data Import Export Framework

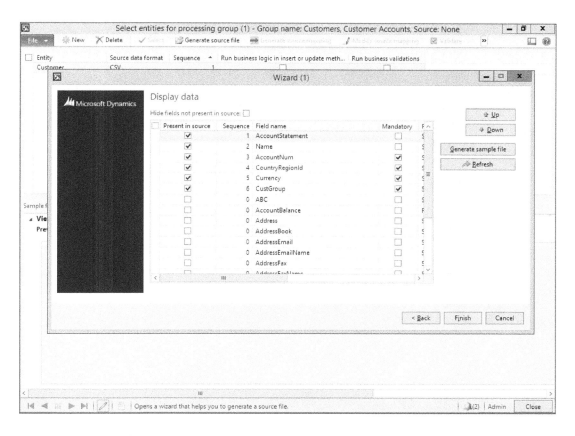

This will take you to the default **Display Data** for the customer entity.

Importing Customers Using The Data Import Export Framework

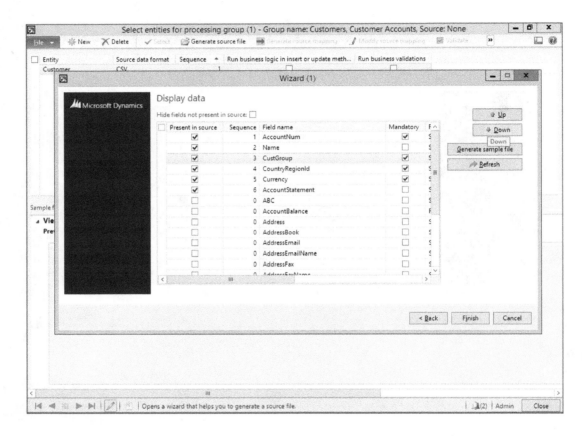

Use the **Up** and **Down** buttons to rearrange the data order - I like the Account Number first.

Importing Customers Using The Data Import Export Framework

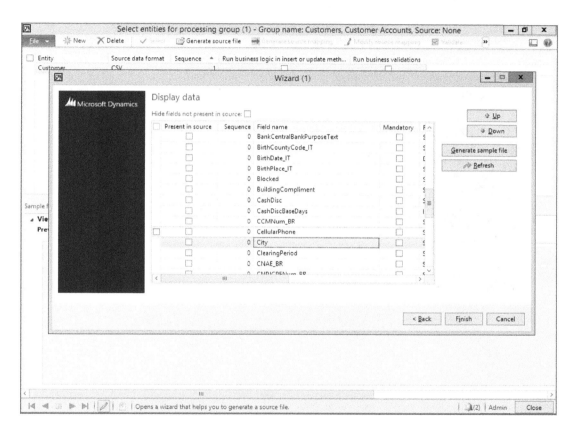

Now search through the unselected fields for the **City** field and then click the **Present In Source** checkbox.

Importing Customers Using The Data Import Export Framework

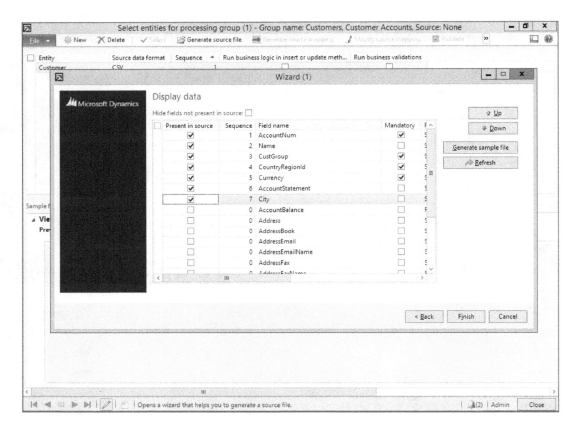

This will add it to the selected mapping fields.

Importing Customers Using The Data Import Export Framework

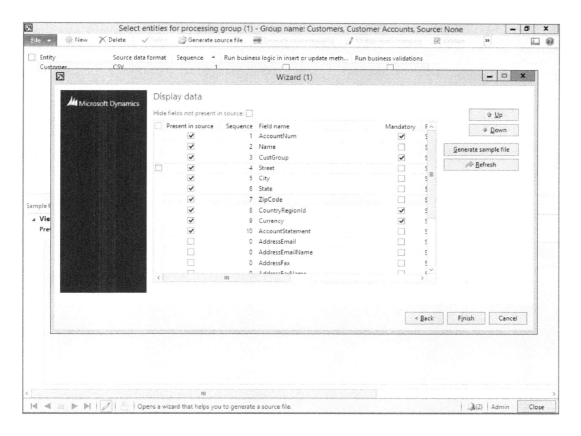

Do the same for the **Street, City, State, Postal Code** and any other additional fields, and then re-order them so that they are more logically grouped.

When you have all of the data points that you want to track against the customer, click on the **Generate Sample File** button to the right of the form.

Importing Customers Using The Data Import Export Framework

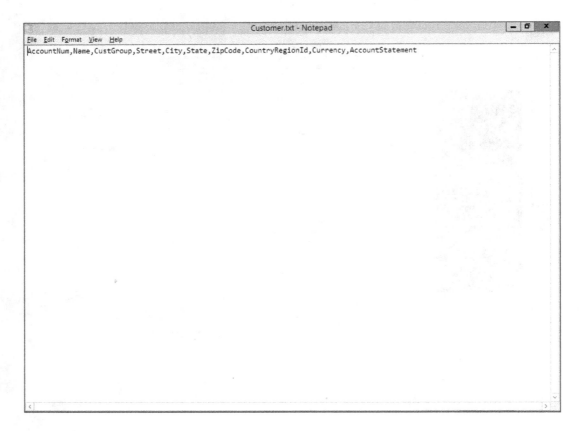

This will create a CSV file for you with all the default headings.

Importing Customers Using The Data Import Export Framework

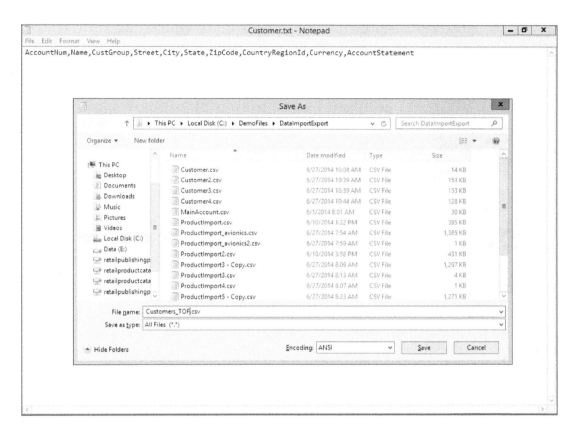

All you need to do is save the file away to a working directory.

Importing Customers Using The Data Import Export Framework

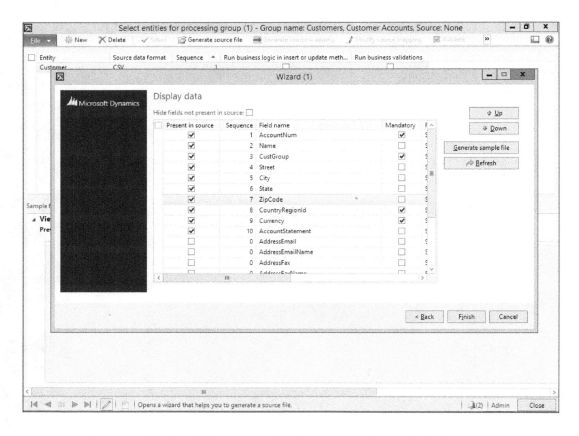

When you have done that, just click on the **Finish** button to exit from the form.

Importing Customers Using The Data Import Export Framework

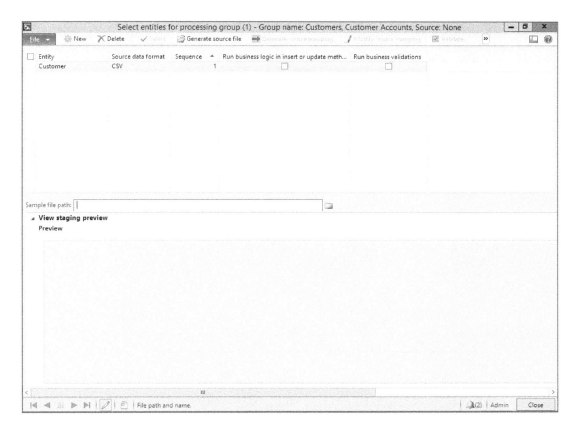

When you return to the **Entities** maintenance form, click on the folder icon to the right of the **Sample File Path** field to open up the file explorer window.

Importing Customers Using The Data Import Export Framework

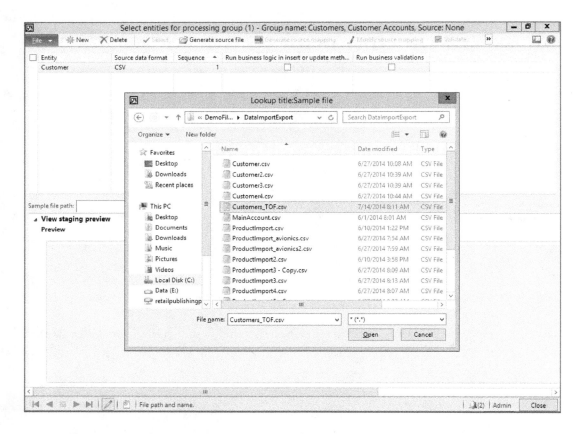

Then point to the new sample CSV file that you just created and click on the **Open** button.

Importing Customers Using The Data Import Export Framework

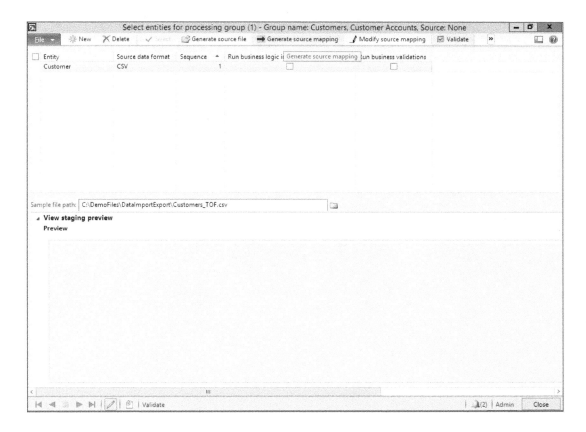

Now you will be able to see the full path to the sample file.

The final task that you need to do is make sure that all of the fields are linked correctly. To do this. Click on the **Generate Source Mapping** button in the menu bar.

Importing Customers Using The Data Import Export Framework

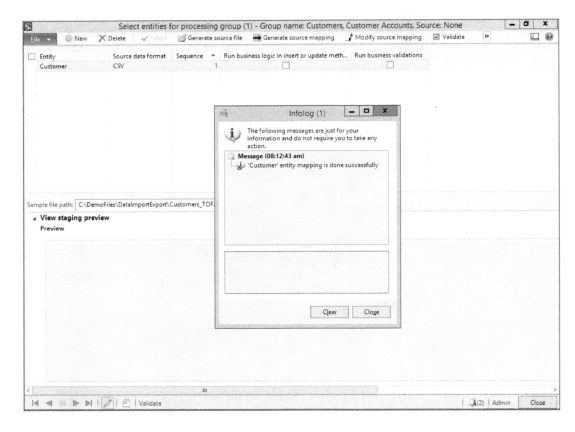

If the sample file matches that entity fields (which there is no reason why it shouldn't) then you will get a simple InfoLog message saying that everything worked great.

Importing Customers Using The Data Import Export Framework

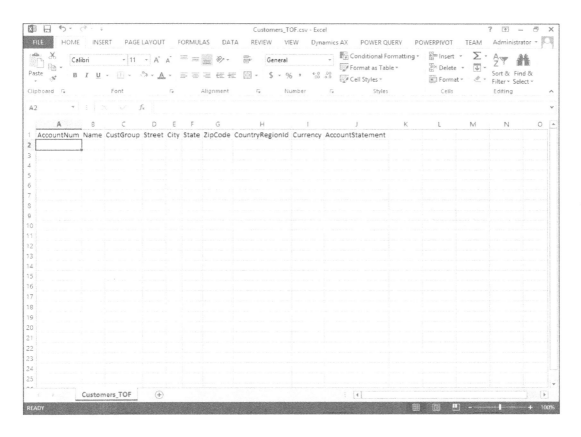

Now we want to start populating our sample file with our customer details. To do this open up the sample file that you created in Excel.

Importing Customers Using The Data Import Export Framework

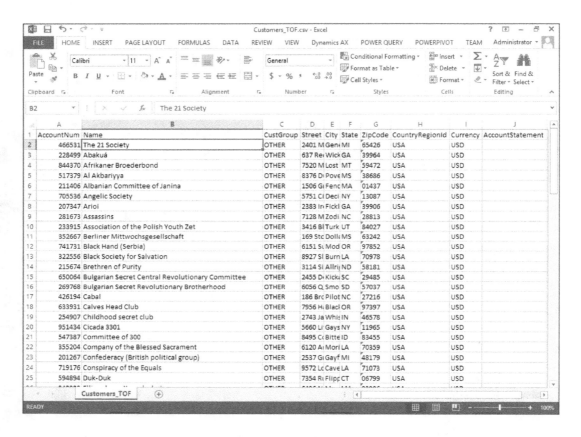

All you need to do is paste in the customer information into the form and define all of the key information.

After you have done that just save the CSV file.

Importing Customers Using The Data Import Export Framework

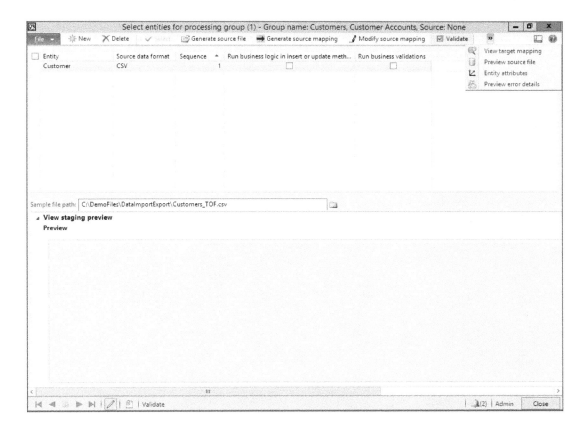

If you want to check that the data file that you created works then click on the **Preview Source File** menu item within the **Entities** maintenance form.

Importing Customers Using The Data Import Export Framework

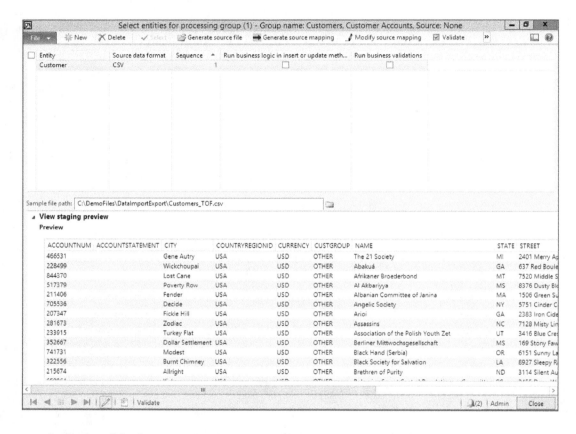

In the footer of the form you should see that all of the data is loading. If it doesn't load then you have a formatting problem with your source data.

If everything looks good then just click the **Close** button to exit from the form.

Importing Customers Using The Data Import Export Framework

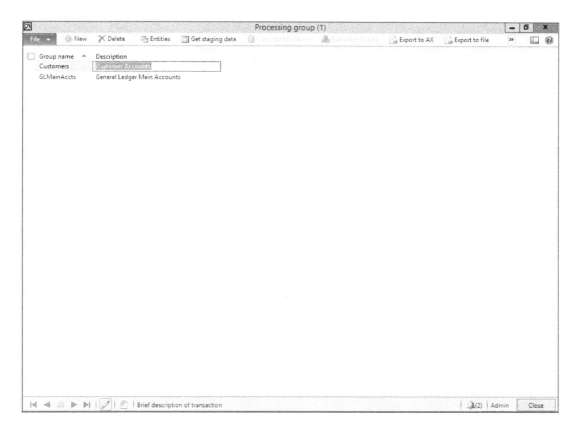

When you return to the **Processing Group** form, you will be able to click on the **Get Staging Data** button in the menu bar.

Importing Customers Using The Data Import Export Framework

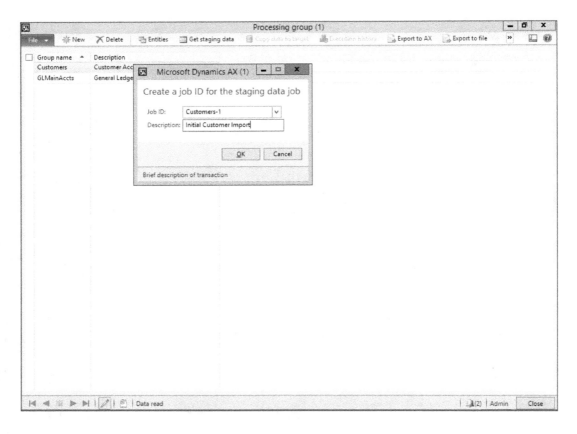

When the **Create Job** dialog box is displayed, you can add some commentary on the job by adding a description and then click on the **OK** button.

Importing Customers Using The Data Import Export Framework

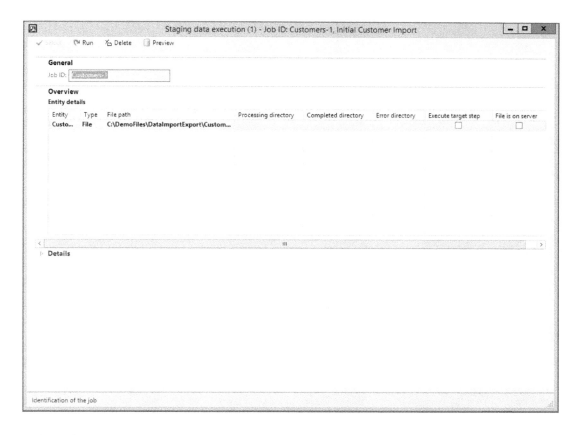

This will open up the **Staging Data Execution** dialog box. If you want to be double sure that the data that you put in the CSV file is good then click on the **Preview** button within the menu bar.

Importing Customers Using The Data Import Export Framework

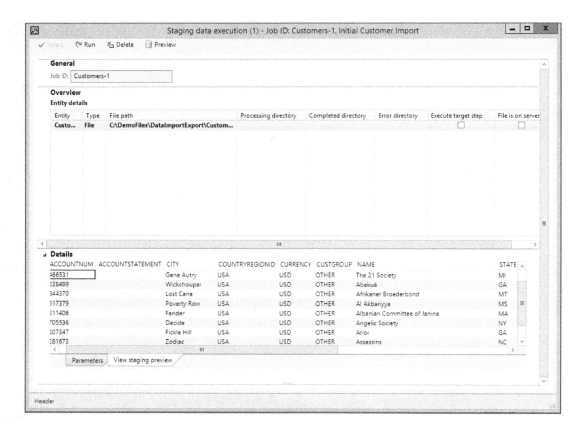

This will show you the staging data based off the import file that you created within the **Details** tab group.

Now just click the **Run** button in the menu bar.

Importing Customers Using The Data Import Export Framework

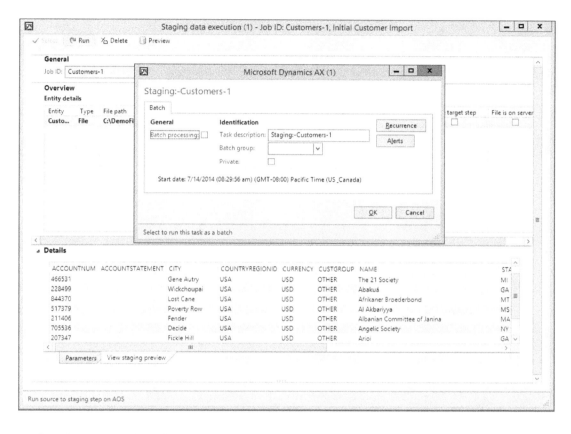

When the **Staging** dialog box is displayed, click on the **OK** button.

Importing Customers Using The Data Import Export Framework

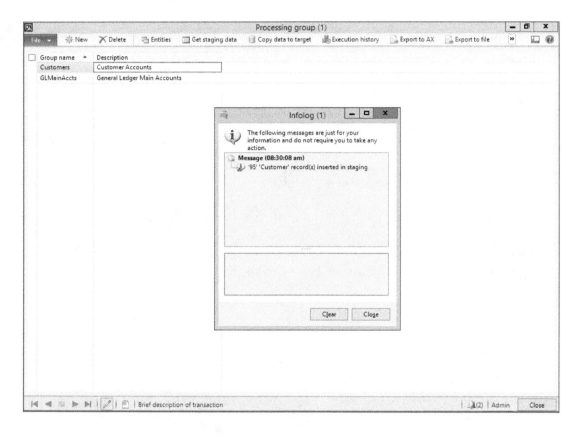

If everything went OK, then you will get an InfoLog box telling you how many records were loaded into the staging area.

Importing Customers Using The Data Import Export Framework

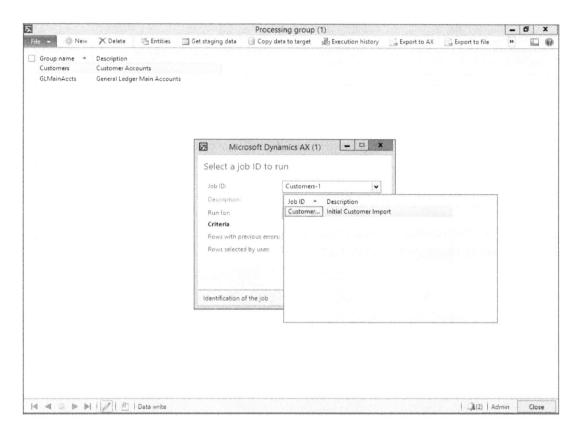

Now you just need to move them into the real customers table by clicking on the **Copy Data To Target** button in the menu bar.

This will open up a selection dialog box and you can select the Job that you want to import into Dynamics AX.

Importing Customers Using The Data Import Export Framework

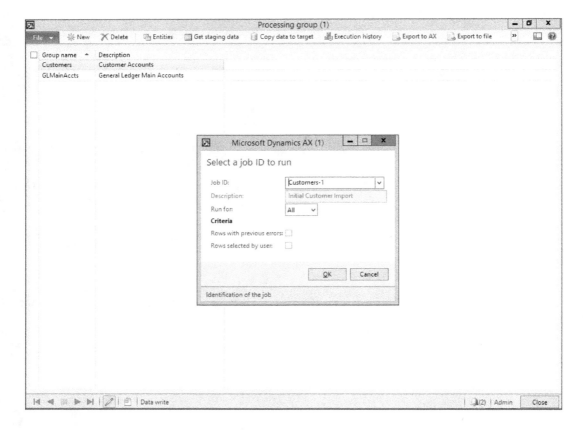

After yyou have selected the job, just click on the **OK** button.

Importing Customers Using The Data Import Export Framework

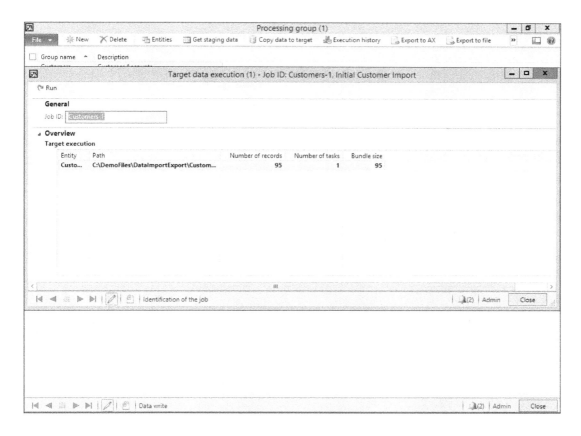

When the **Target Data Execution** dialog box is displayed, click on the **Run** button in the menu bar.

Importing Customers Using The Data Import Export Framework

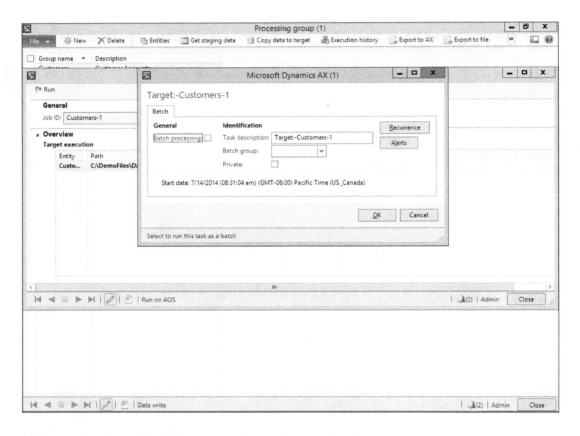

Then click on the **OK** button when the **Target** dialog box is displayed.

Importing Customers Using The Data Import Export Framework

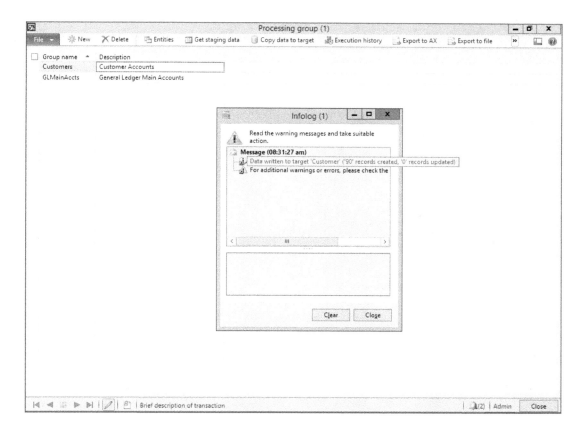

If everything went according to plan you will get an InfoLog message saying that the data was copied into Dynamics AX.

Importing Customers Using The Data Import Export Framework

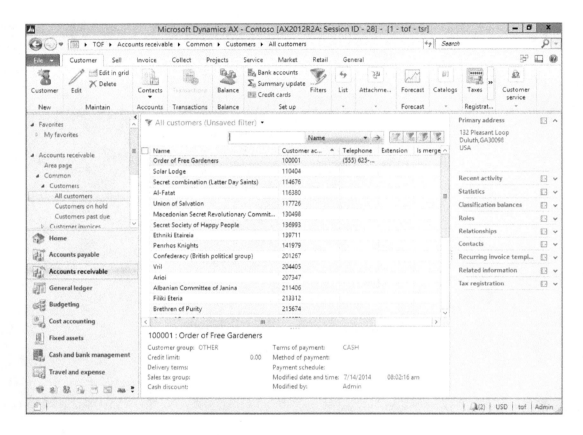

If you open up the **All Customers** list page you will see all of the new records are waiting there for you.

Importing Customers Using The Data Import Export Framework

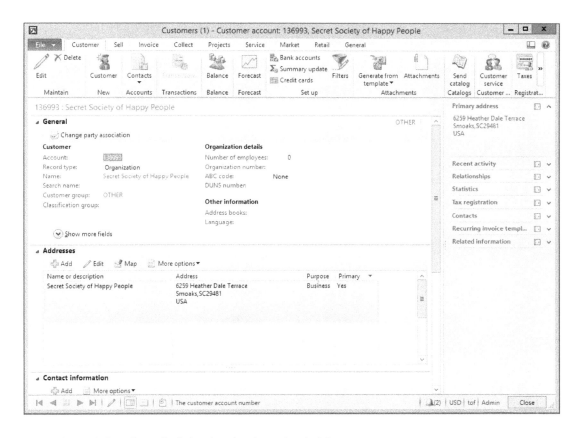

And if you drill in then all of the data has been loaded for you.

How easy is that?

Updating Customer Information Manually

If you didn't catch all of the fields that you needed to when you imported in all of your customers, then you may need to polish the records a little by hand. There are a number of different ways that you can do this, but for small changes sometimes it's just easier to fo directly to the record and make the update.

Updating Customer Information Manually

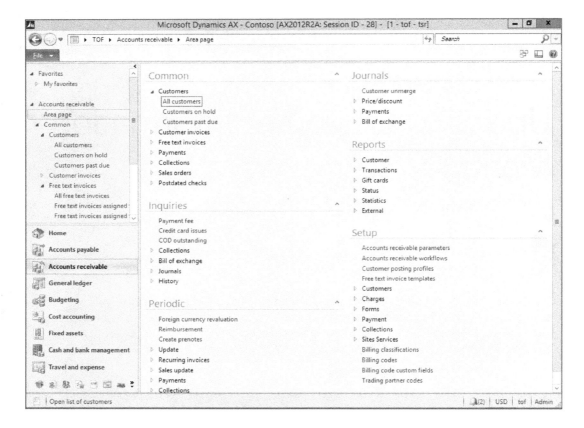

To do this, click on the **All Customers** menu item within the **Customers** folder of the **Common** group of the **Accounts Receivable** area page.

Updating Customer Information Manually

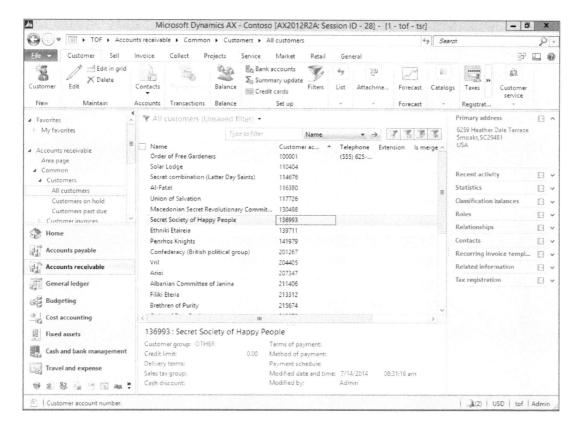

When the **Customers** list page is displayed, double click on the customer record that you want to change.

Updating Customer Information Manually

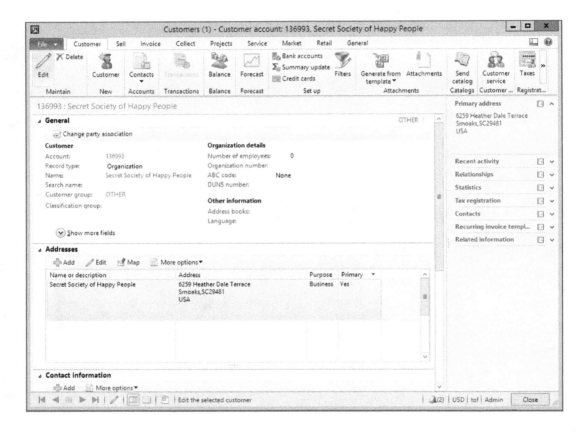

This will open up the **Customer** detail page. Click on the **Edit** button within the **Maintain** group of the **Customer** ribbon bar.

Updating Customer Information Manually

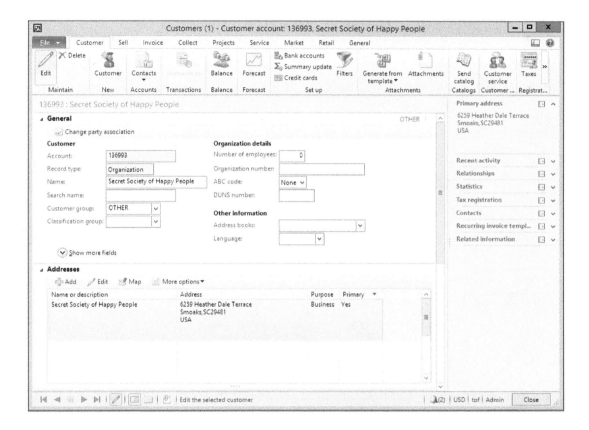

Now you will be in edit mode and you can make changes.

Updating Customer Information Manually

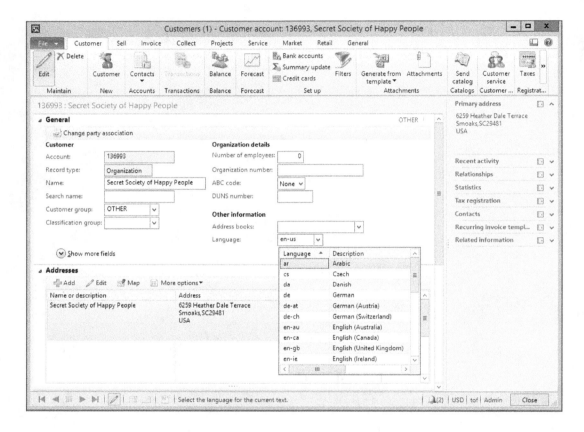

For example, one change that you may want to make is to set the **Language** for the customer.

Updating Customer Information Manually

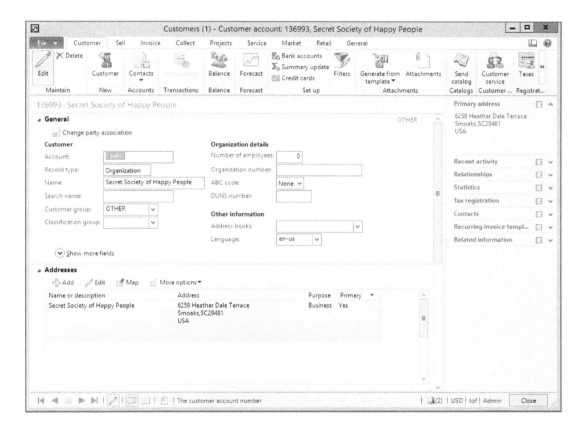

Once you have made the change you can save the record and then click the **Close** button to exit out of the detail form.

Performing Bulk Updates Using The Edit In Grid Function

If you need to make the same change to a number of records at once, then you can use the **Edit In Grid** function to update the records in more of a spreadsheet format.

Performing Bulk Updates Using The Edit In Grid Function

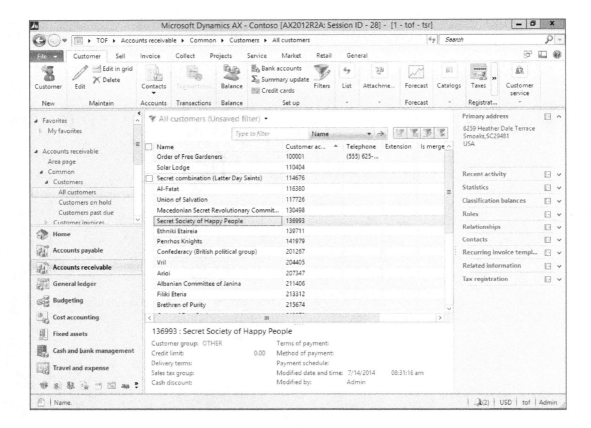

To do this, open up the **All Customers** list page, and then click on the **Edit In Grid** button within the **Maintain** group of the **Customers** ribbon bar.

Performing Bulk Updates Using The Edit In Grid Function

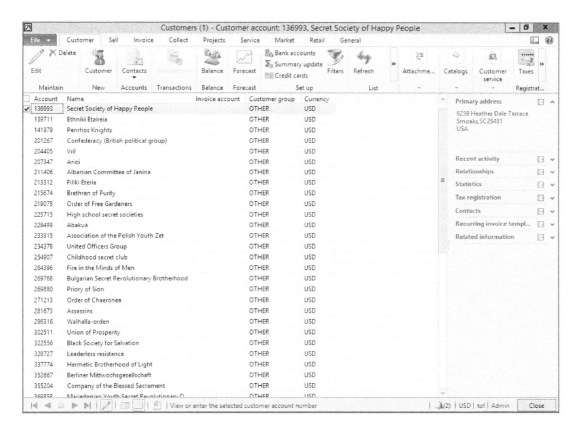

This will switch you to a new grid view with default fields for the customer record.

Performing Bulk Updates Using The Edit In Grid Function

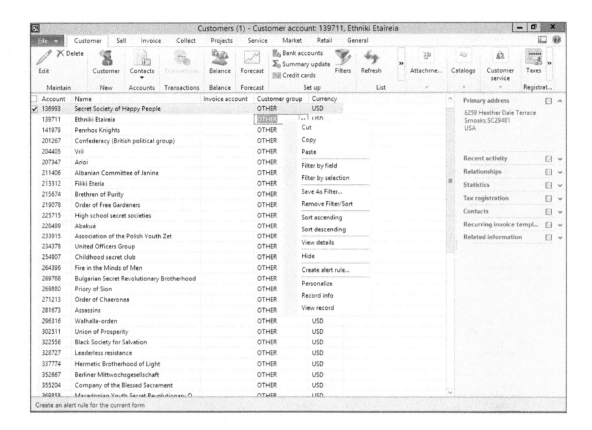

One thing that you will notice about this view is that you can update any of the fields you like here and navigate up, down, left and right within the data.

If there is a field that you want to update though that is not on the form then you can add it to the grid by right-mouse-clicking on the table and selecting the **Personalize** option.

Performing Bulk Updates Using The Edit In Grid Function

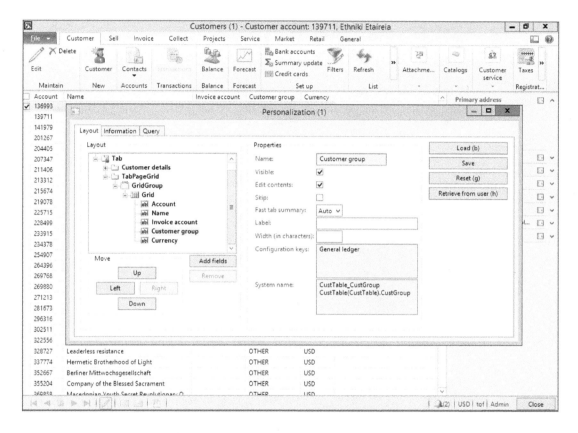

When the **Personalization** form is displayed, click on the **Add Fields** button.

Performing Bulk Updates Using The Edit In Grid Function

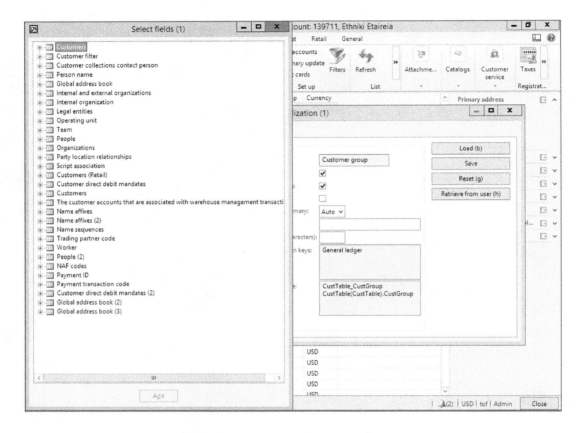

This will open up the Field Selection list showing you all of the tables that are linked to the grid page. Expand out the **Global Address Book** group by double clicking on it.

Performing Bulk Updates Using The Edit In Grid Function

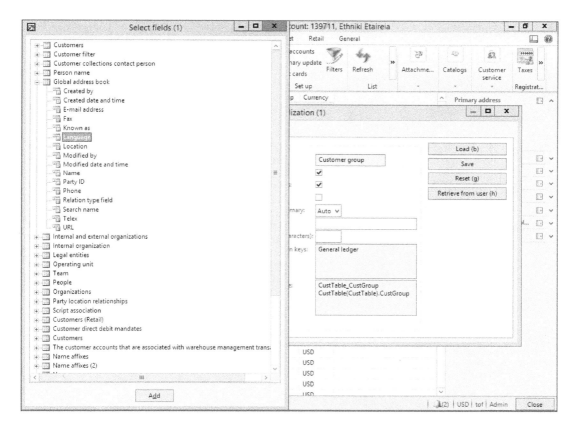

Now you will see all of the fields that are available within that group. Select the **Language** field and click on the **Add** button to add it to the grid page and then close the form.

Performing Bulk Updates Using The Edit In Grid Function

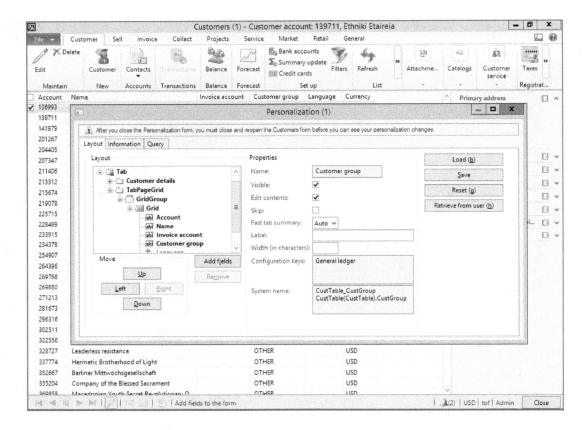

Now you will see that the **Language** field has been added to the grid definition and you can close the **Personalization** form.

Performing Bulk Updates Using The Edit In Grid Function

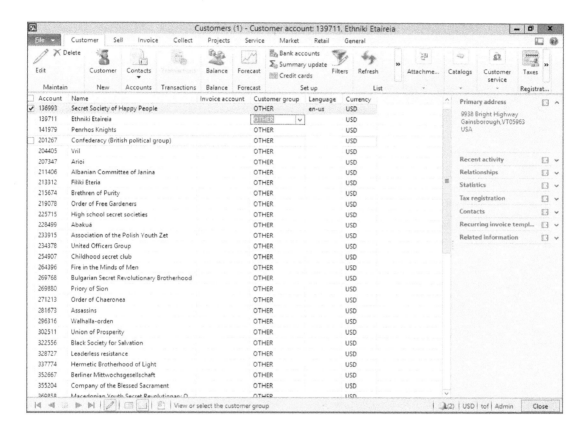

When you return to the grid page you will see that the **Language** field has been added.

Performing Bulk Updates Using The Edit In Grid Function

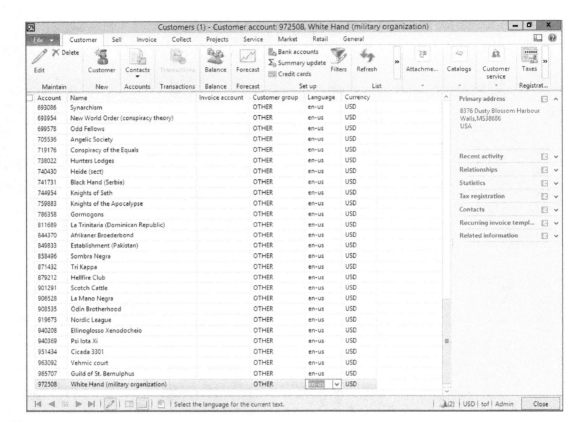

To update all of the records just cut and paste down the grid until you have updated all of the records.

Performing Mass Updates Using Excel

Sometimes you don't need to polish your customer records so much as chisel larger chunks of data. An easy way to do this is to use Excel as the data update tool because you can perform mass updates quickly through cut and pasting data.

Performing Mass Updates Using Excel

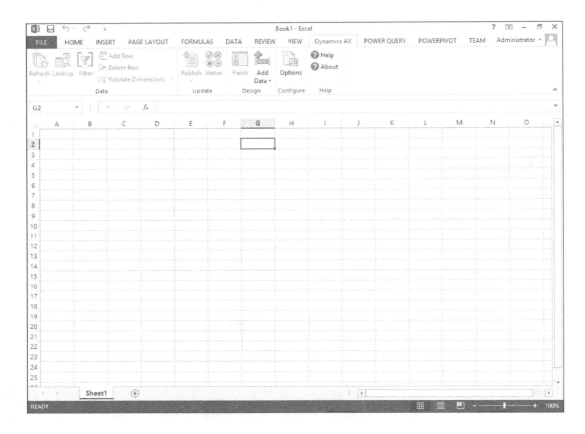

To do this open up Excel and switch to the **Dynamics AX** ribbon bar.

Performing Mass Updates Using Excel

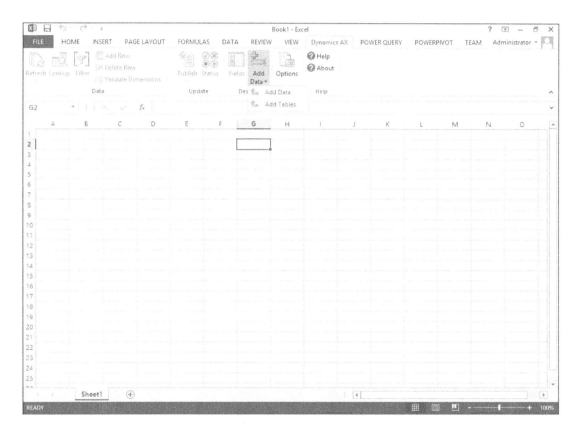

Then click on the **Add Data** button within the **Design** group of the **Dynamics AX** ribbon bar and select the **Add Tables** menu item.

Performing Mass Updates Using Excel

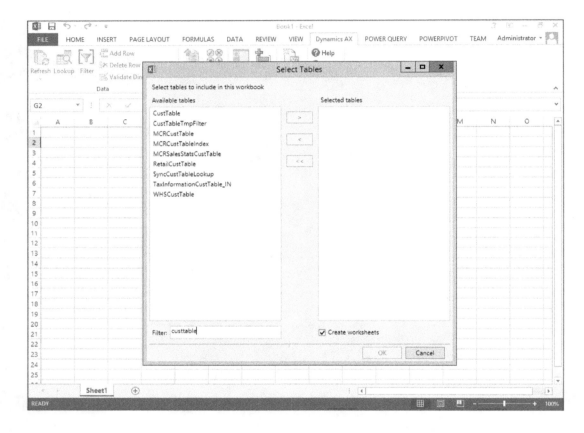

When the **Select Tables** dialog box is displayed, filter out the tables by typing **CustTable** into the **Filter** field.

Performing Mass Updates Using Excel

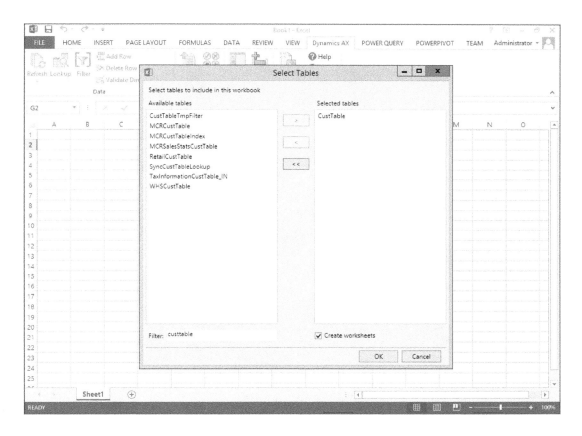

Select the **CustTable** table and click on the **>** button to add it to the **Selected Tables** group and then click on the **OK** button.

Performing Mass Updates Using Excel

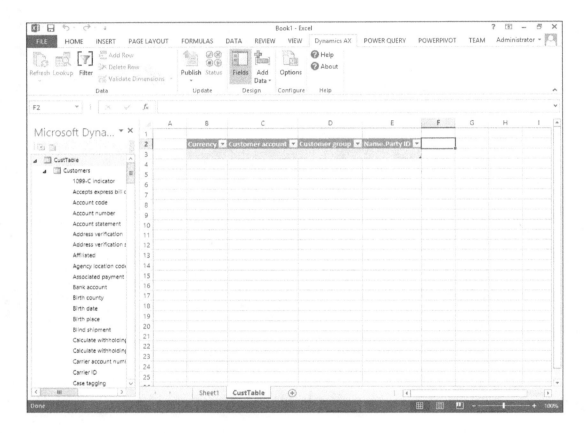

This will create a worksheet for you that is linked to the **CustTable** table and also add the main index fields to the worksheet.

Performing Mass Updates Using Excel

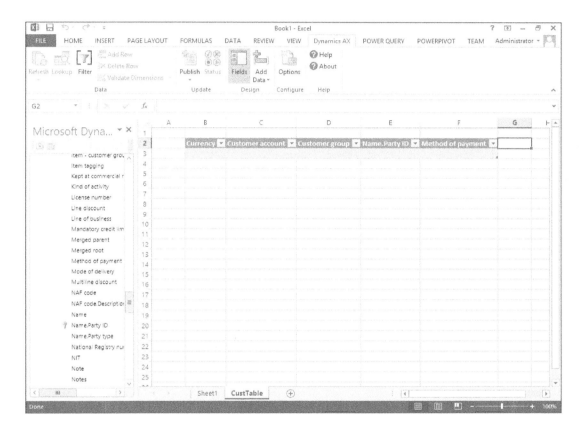

You can drag additional fields from the field chooser onto the worksheet – in this case we will add the **Method Of Payment** field so that we can update it.

When you have added all of the fields that you want to update, click on the **Fields** button within the **Design** group of the **Dynamics AX** ribbon bar.

Performing Mass Updates Using Excel

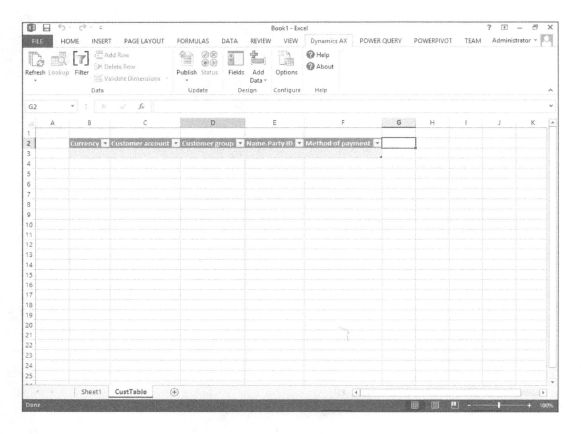

This will switch you out of design mode into edit. Before we start updating the data thought, click on the **Options** button within the **Configure** group of the **Dynamics AX** ribbon bar.

Performing Mass Updates Using Excel

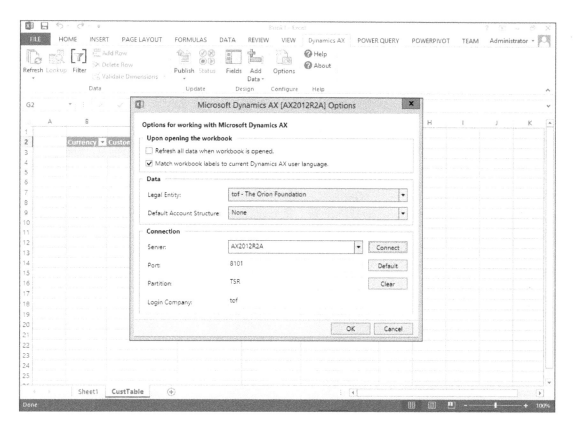

When the **Options** dialog box is displayed, make sure that you are connected to the right partition and company. If it looks good then click on the **OK** button.

Performing Mass Updates Using Excel

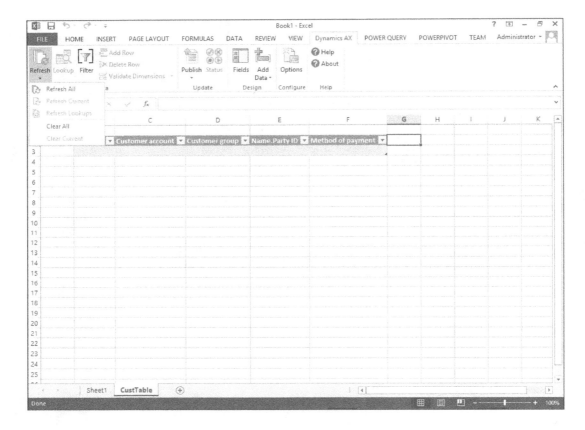

Now click on the **Refresh** button within the **Data** group of the **Dynamics AX** ribbon bar and select the **Refresh All** menu item.

Performing Mass Updates Using Excel

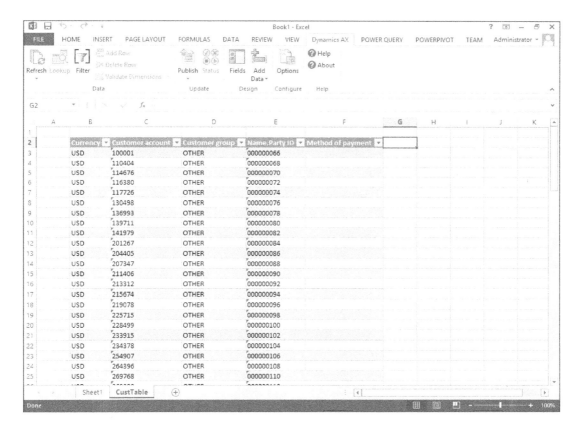

This will populate all of the customer data within the worksheet for you.

Performing Mass Updates Using Excel

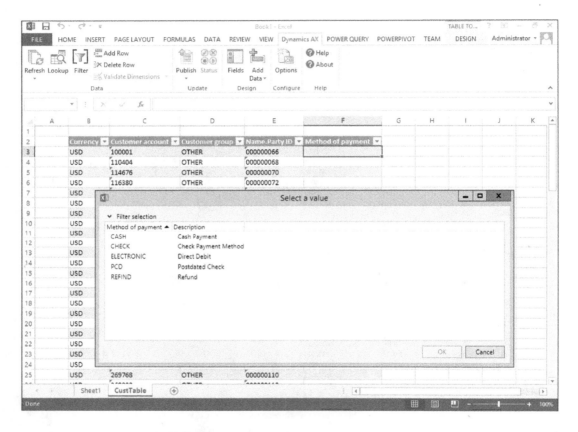

Select the first **Method Of Payment** cell and then click on the **Lookup** button within the **Data** group of the **Dynamics AX** ribbon bar.

This will show you all of the valid methods of payment that you have configured within **Dynamics AX** and you can select one of them by double clicking on it.

Performing Mass Updates Using Excel

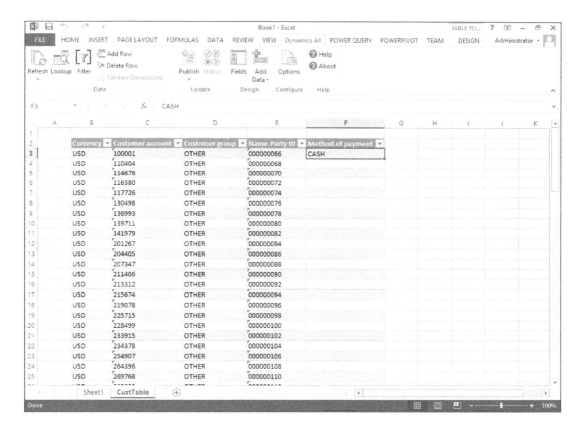

And now the Method Of Payment cell will have the selected value.

Performing Mass Updates Using Excel

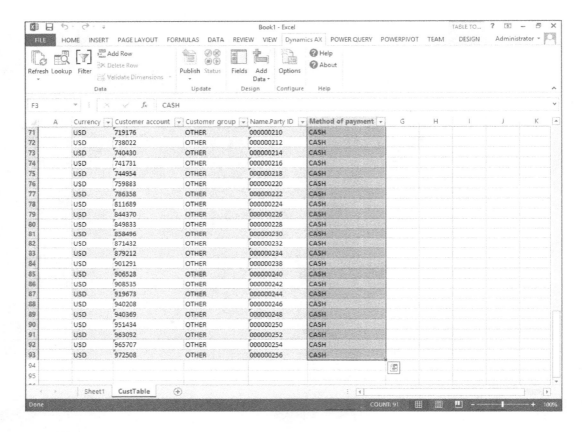

The major benefit of using Excel is that you can fill down though all of the rows in one simple step.

Performing Mass Updates Using Excel

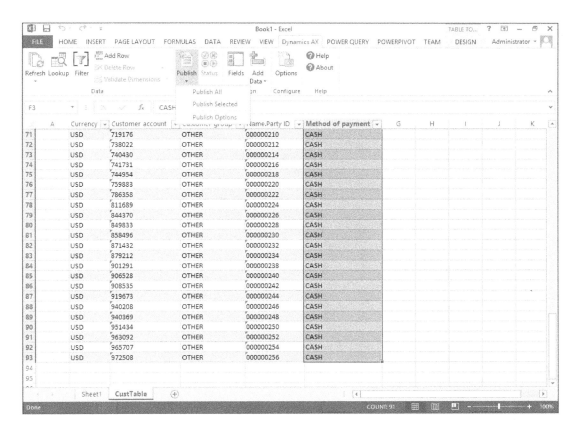

To update **Dynamics AX** all you need to do is click on the **Publish** button within the **Update** group of the **Dynamics AX** ribbon bar and select the **Publish All** menu item.

Performing Mass Updates Using Excel

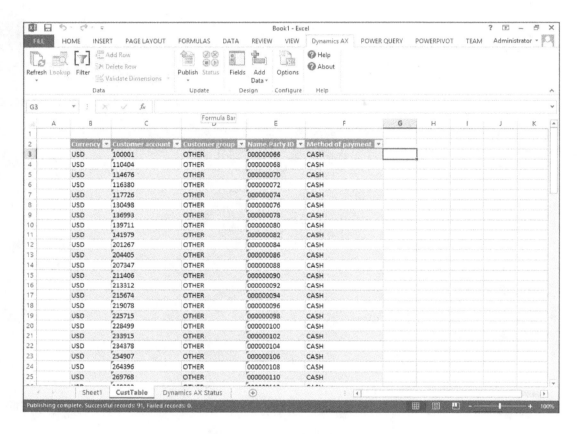

After a couple of seconds, all of the data will be updated.

Performing Mass Updates Using Excel

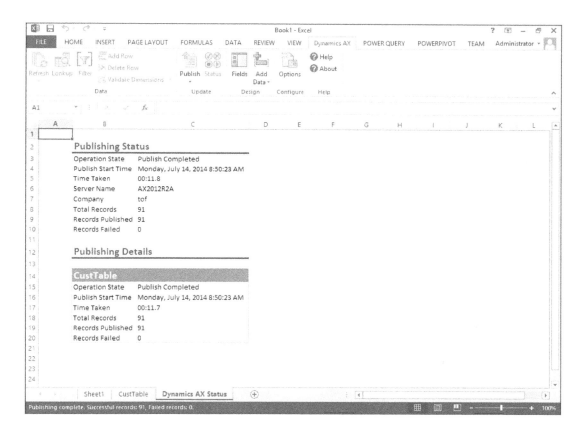

You will also notice that a new tab is added to the workbook, which shows you how many records were updated, and how long the update took. This is more useful if there are errors because it will show you the Dynamics AX errors listed by record.

Performing Mass Updates Using Excel

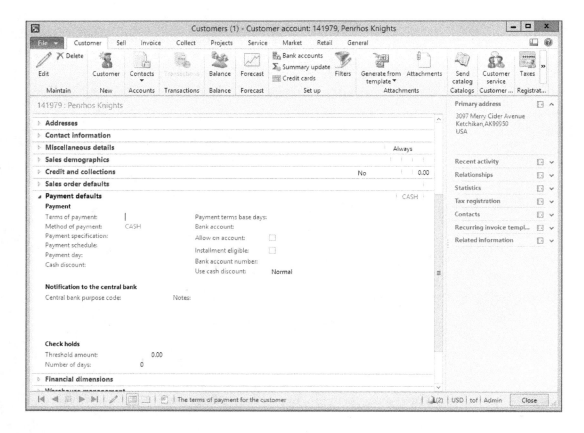

Now if we return to our Customer record then we will also see that the fields have been updated.

How easy is that!

CONFIGURING INVOICING

Now that we have the customers configured we can start getting down to business and doing some invoicing. There are a number of different invoicing options within Dynamics AX and in this section we will walk through the main ones.

Entering A Free Text Invoice

The simplest type of invoice that we can create is a **Free Text Invoice** which allows you to invoice pretty much anything that you like.

Entering A Free Text Invoice

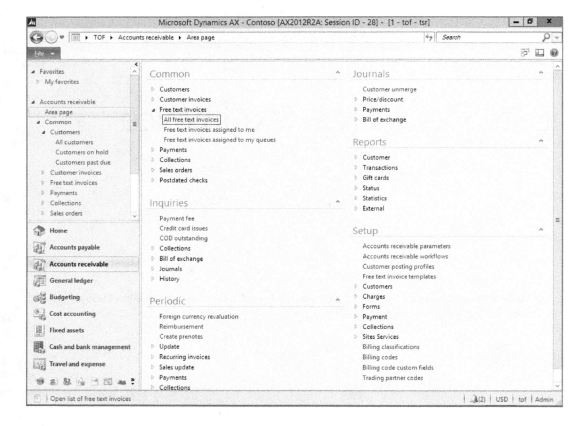

To do this, click on the **All Free Text Invoices** menu item within the **Free Text Invoices** folder of the **Common** group within the **Accounts Receivable** area page.

Entering A Free Text Invoice

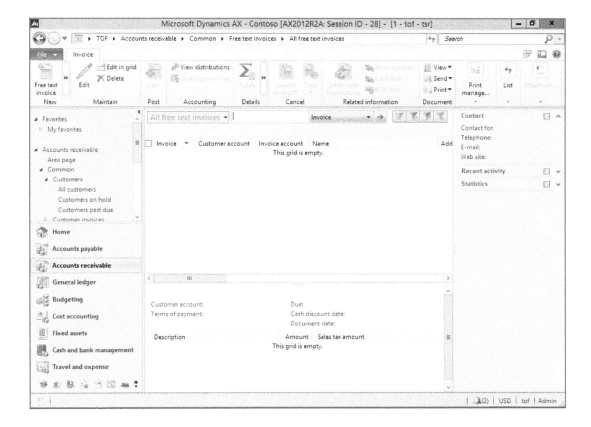

When the **Free Text Invoice** list page is displayed, click on the **Free Text Invoice** menu button within the **New** group of the **Invoice** ribbon bar to create a new record.

Entering A Free Text Invoice

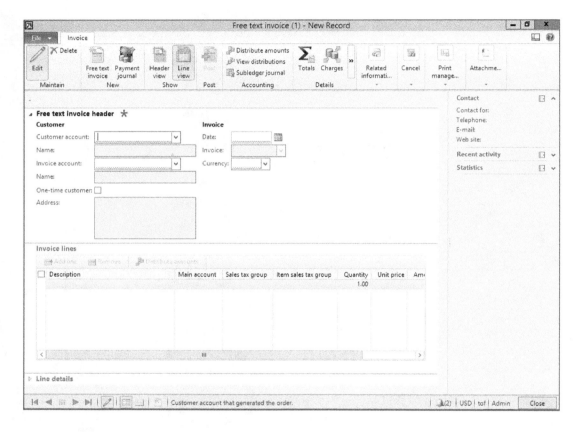

This will open up the **Free Text Invoice** details form.

Entering A Free Text Invoice

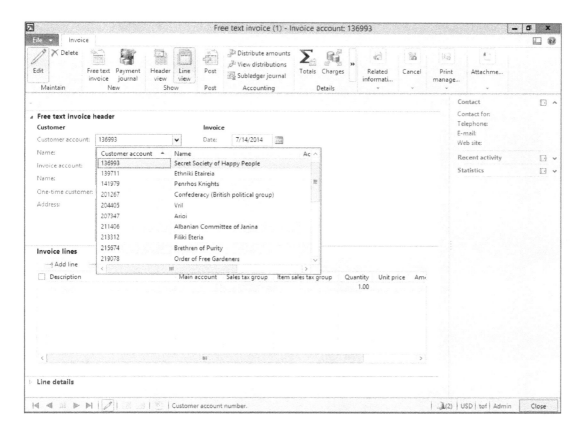

From the **Customer Account** dropdown list, select the customer that you want to create the invoice for.

Entering A Free Text Invoice

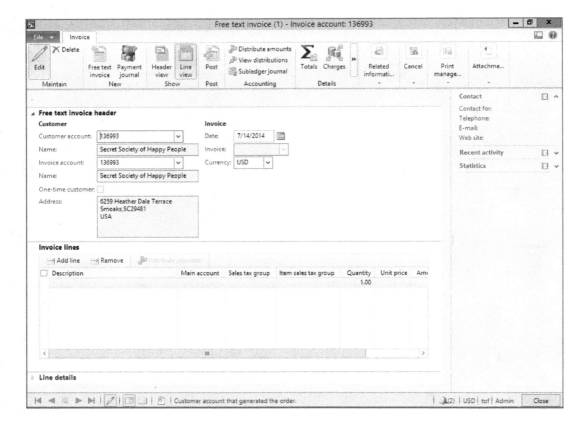

After you have selected your customer, notice that the **Invoice Account** defaults in as the same as the customer account. If you want to send the bill to another parent account then you can change the **Invoice Account** right here.

Entering A Free Text Invoice

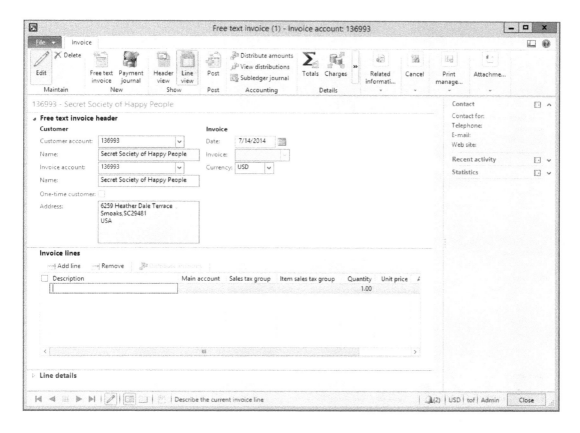

Now click on the **Add Line** button within the **Invoice Lines** grid to add an invoice line.

Entering A Free Text Invoice

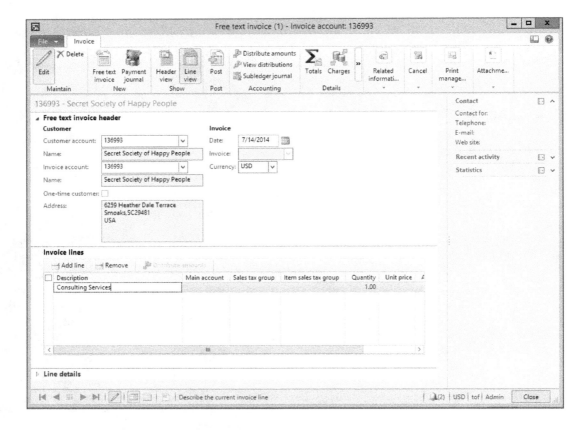

Enter a **Description** for what you want to invoice.

Entering A Free Text Invoice

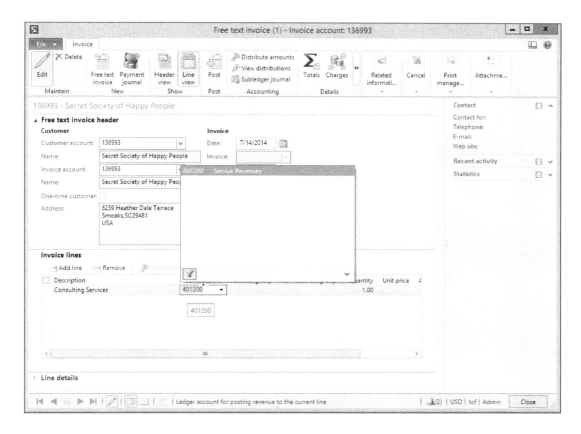

Then from the **Main Account** dropdown list, select the account that you want the invoice line to post to.

Entering A Free Text Invoice

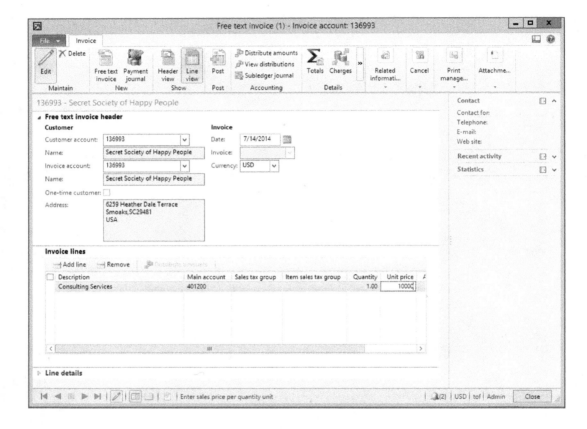

Now you can update the **Quantity** and the **Unit Price** for the invoice line to get the extended amount.

Entering A Free Text Invoice

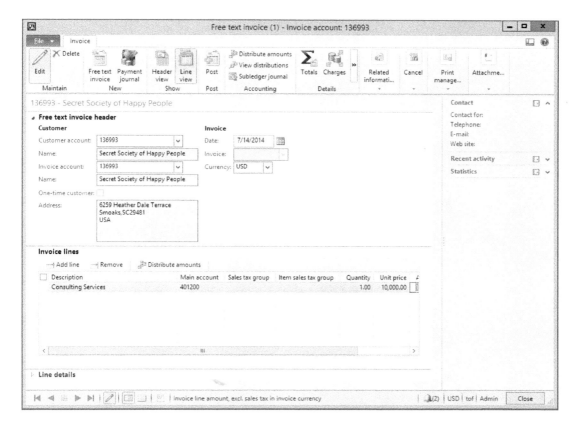

Once you are done, you can save the invoice and move on to the next one if you like.

Posting Free Text Invoices

Once you have created your Free Text Invoice and want it to become a live invoice within the system, all you need to do it post it.

Posting Free Text Invoices

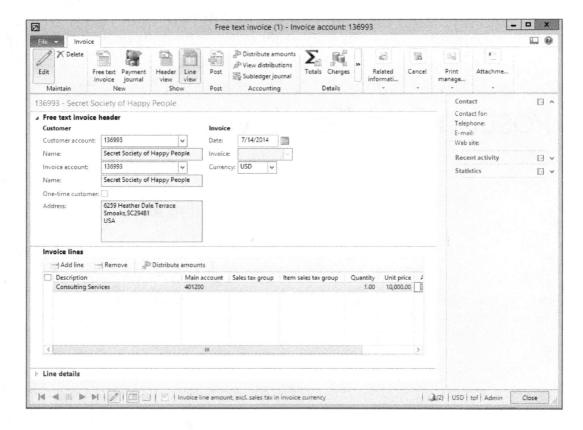

To do this open up your **Free Text Invoice** and click on the **Post** button within the **Post** group of the **Invoice** ribbon bar.

Posting Free Text Invoices

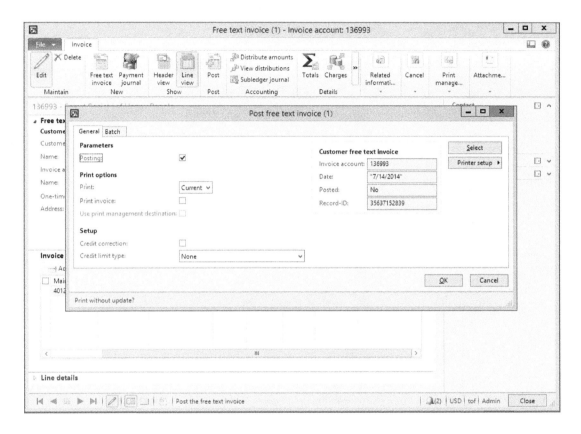

This will open up the **Post Free Text Invoice** dialog box, and all you need to do is click on the **OK** button.

Posting Free Text Invoices

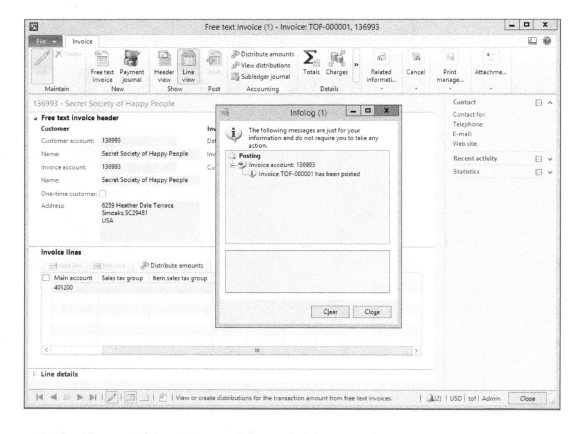

You should get an InfoLog message telling you that the invoice has posted.

Rock on!

Viewing Journal Information From Posted Invoices

All of the actual postings and transactions within the GL have been hidden away from you while you have been entering your Free Text Invoice, but if you really want to view the transactions then that's not a problem.

Viewing Journal Information From Posted Invoices

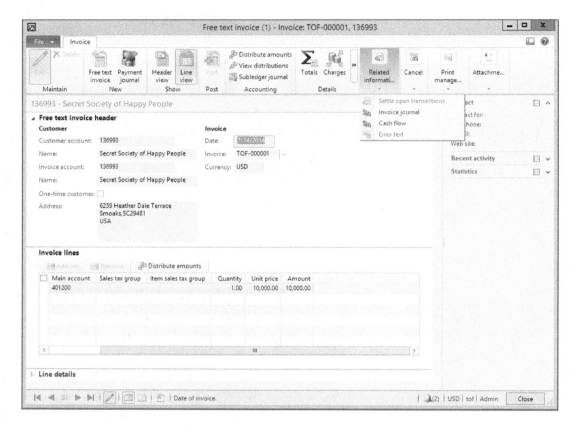

To do this, open up your posted Free Text Invoice and click on the **Invoice Journal** button within the **Related Information** group of the **Invoice** ribbon bar.

Viewing Journal Information From Posted Invoices

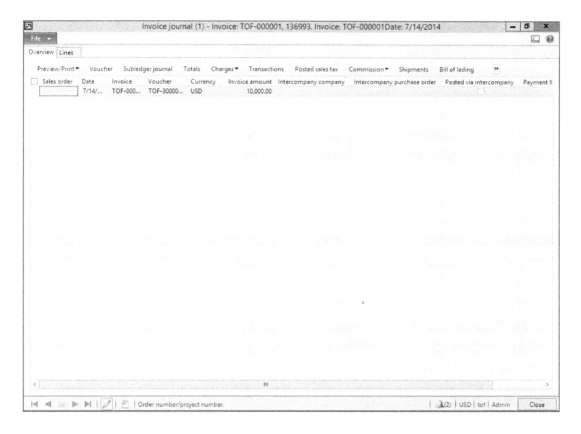

This will take you straight to the journal that was created for the invoice.

Viewing Journal Information From Posted Invoices

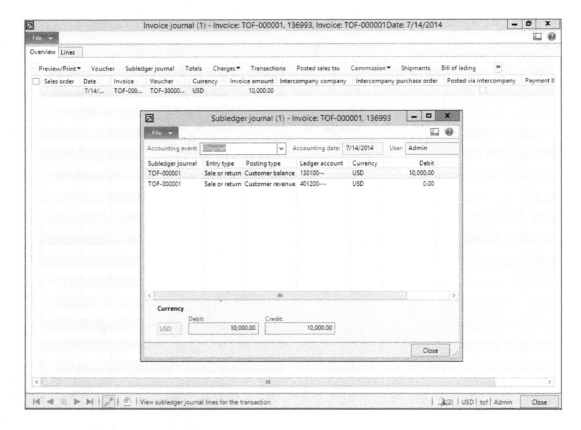

If you want to see all of the postings that were created within the sub-ledger, click on the **Subledger Journal** button in the menu bar.

Reprinting Posted Invoices From The Invoice Journal

If you ever need to reprint an Invoice for a customer then you can do that directly from the Invoice Journal itself without having to find the original Invoice record.

Reprinting Posted Invoices From The Invoice Journal

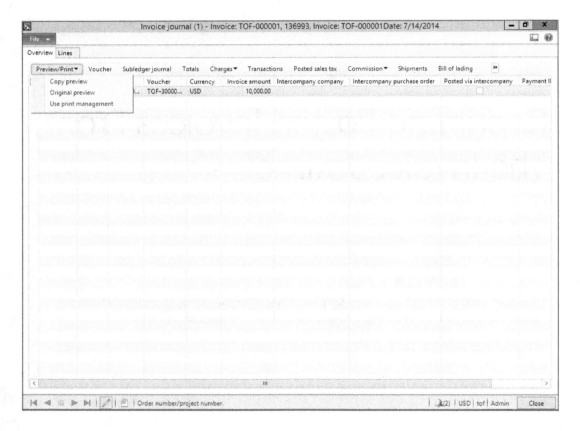

To do this, select the Invoice Journal that you want to reprint the invoice for, click on the **Preview/Print** menu item and then select the type of Invoice that you want to print.

Reprinting Posted Invoices From The Invoice Journal

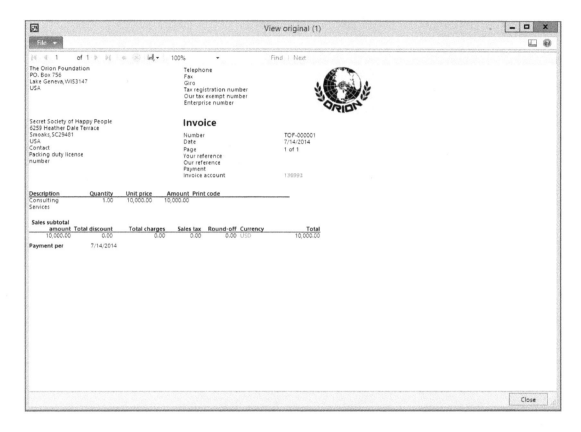

Dynamics AX will then create a preview of the Invoice for you and you can print it, e-mail it, or save it away for later on.

Entering a Free Text Invoice From The Customer Record

There are always a number of different paths that you can take within Dynamics AX to get to the same result, and you just pick the one that is most convenient for you. One example of this is the feature that allows you to generate your free text invoices directly from the Customer record itself. This is a great shortcut if you are already on the customer account and want to invoice them.

Entering a Free Text Invoice From The Customer Record

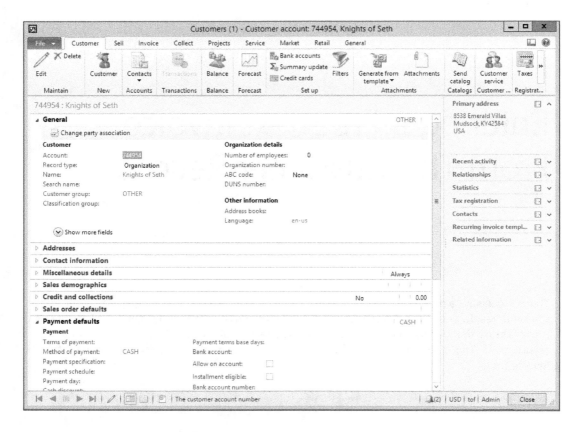

To do this, start off by opening up the customer record.

Entering a Free Text Invoice From The Customer Record

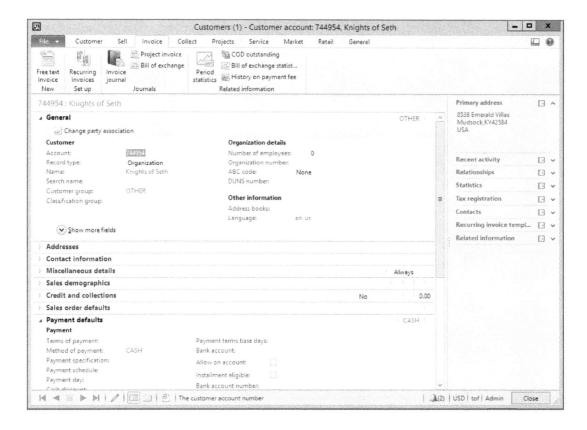

Then switch to the **Invoice** ribbon bar and click on the **Free Text Invoice** menu item within the **New** group.

Entering a Free Text Invoice From The Customer Record

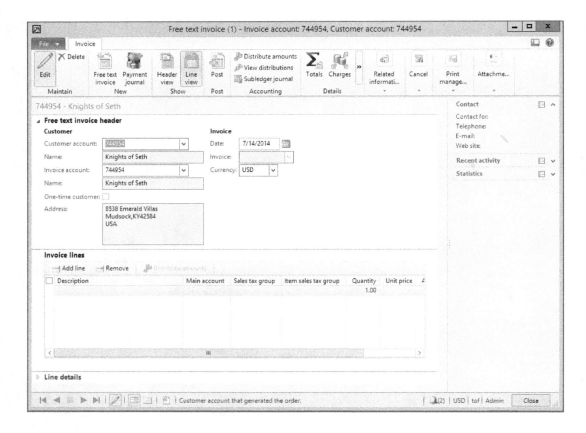

This will take you straight into the **Free Text Invoice** form, and will have pre-populated the **Customer Account** and all of the other default information.

Entering a Free Text Invoice From The Customer Record

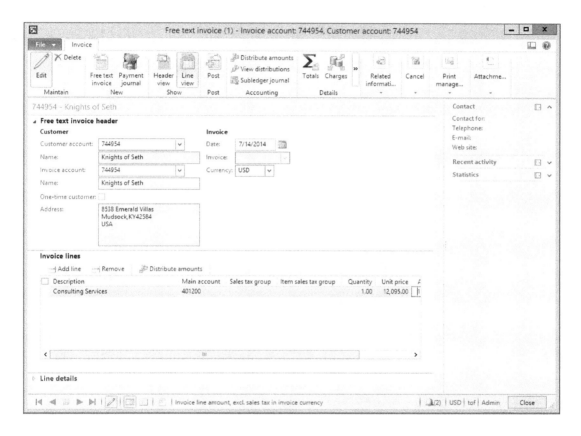

All you need to do is add the Invoice line just like you did earlier.

Entering a Free Text Invoice From The Customer Record

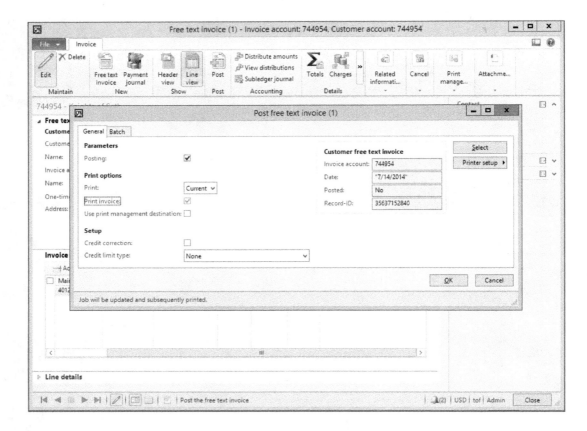

Then click on the **Post** button within the **Post** group of the **Invoice** ribbon bar to open up the **Post Free Text Invoice** dialog box.

If you want to also print the invoice at the same time then check the **Print Invoice** flag before clicking on the **OK** button.

Entering a Free Text Invoice From The Customer Record

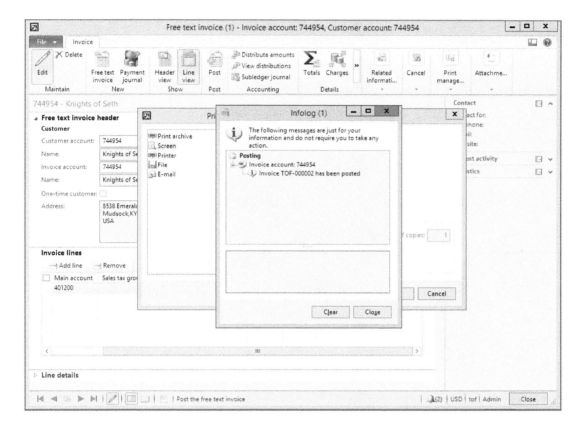

You will then get a InfoLog saying that everything was posted.

Entering a Free Text Invoice From The Customer Record

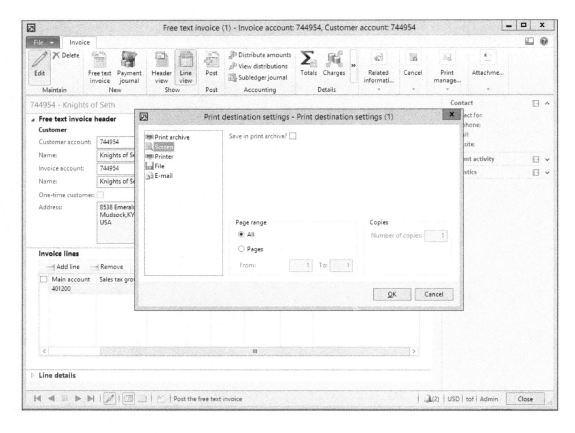

And the **Print Destination Settings** dialog box will also be displayed. To preview the invoice on the screen select the **Screen** option and then click the **OK** button.

Entering a Free Text Invoice From The Customer Record

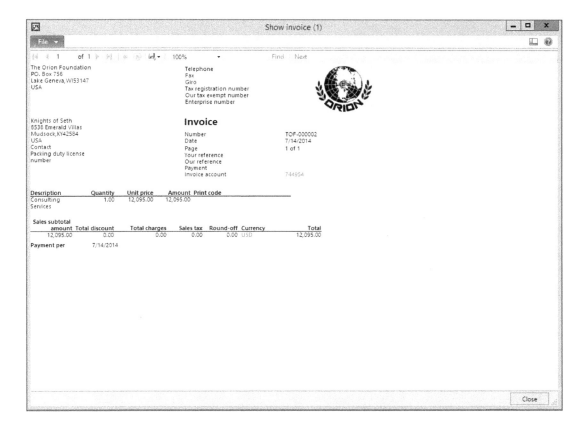

Now you will be able to see the copy of the invoice.

That was pretty darn easy.

CONFIGURING COLLECTION MANAGEMENT

Once you have your invoicing configured you will probably want to set up the Collections Management portion of the Accounts Receivable area. This will allow you to track your customer aging's, pools for segregating customers, collection letters and much more.

Configuring Aging Period Definitions

The first task that we need to do is to configure our aging period definitions.

Configuring Aging Period Definitions

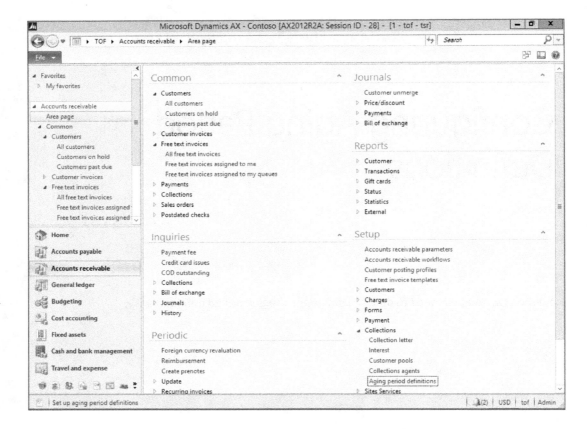

To do this, click on the **Aging Period Definitions** menu item within the **Collections** folder of the **Setup** group of the **Accounts Receivable** area page.

Configuring Aging Period Definitions

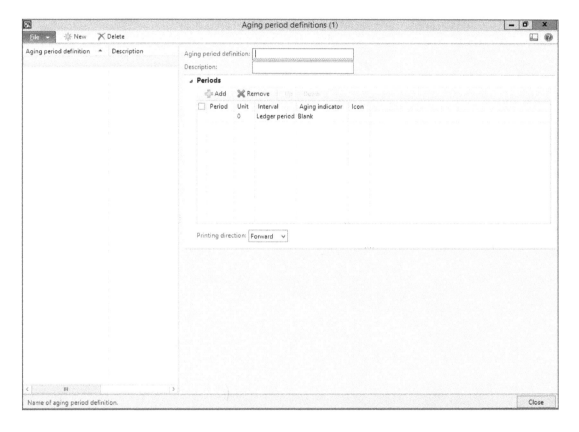

When the **Aging Period Definition** maintenance form is displayed, click on the **New** button in the menu bar to create a new record.

Configuring Aging Period Definitions

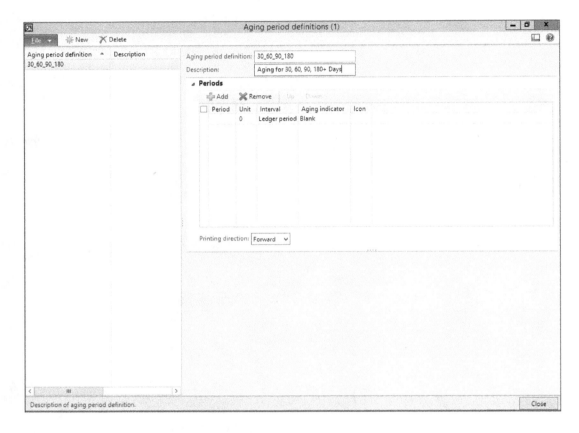

Set the **Aging Period Definition** code to **30_60_90_180** and the **Description** to **Aging for 30, 60, 90, 180+ Days**.

Configuring Aging Period Definitions

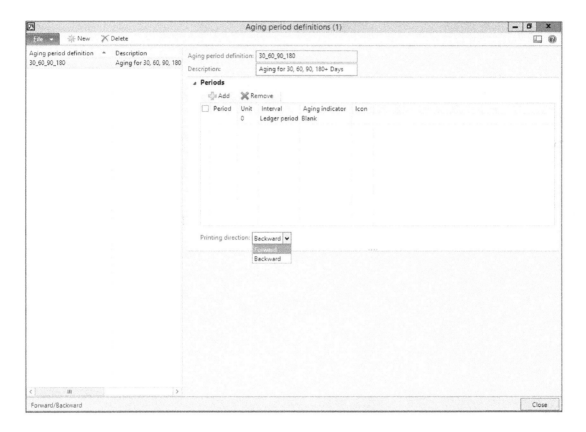

Then set the **Posting** Direction to **Backward** to identify that we will be aging historical dates.

Configuring Aging Period Definitions

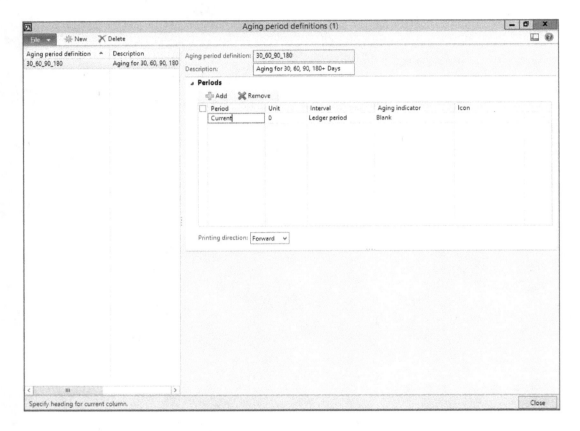

Now we need to create our period buckets. To do this, click on the **Add** button within the **Periods** tab group, and set the **Period** name to be **Current**.

Configuring Aging Period Definitions

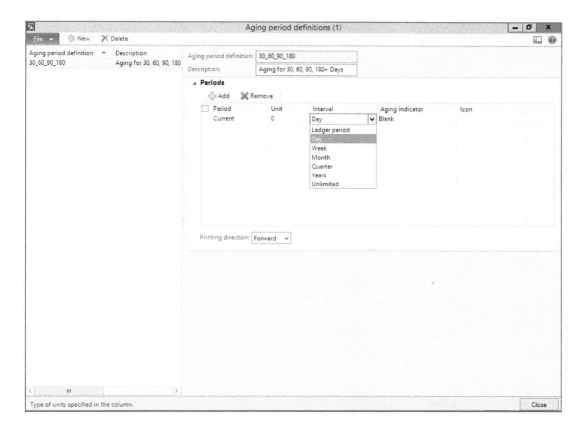

Set the **Interval** to **Day**.

Configuring Aging Period Definitions

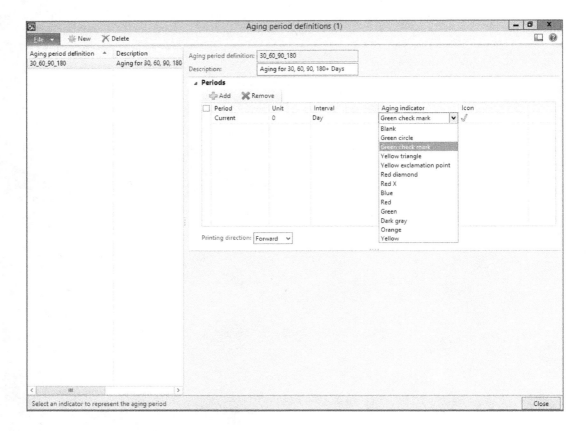

And then select the **Green Check Mark** icon from the **Aging Indicator** dropdown list.

Configuring Aging Period Definitions

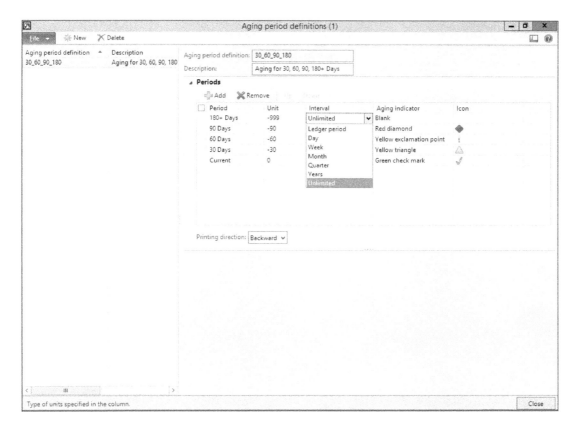

Repeat the process for the **30, 60,** and **90 Days** periods, except set the **Unit** field to **-30, -60,** and **-90** respectively.

For the final **180+ Days** aging bucket, set the **Unit** to **-999** and the **Interval** to **Unlimited** to make it a catch all bucket.

Configuring Aging Period Definitions

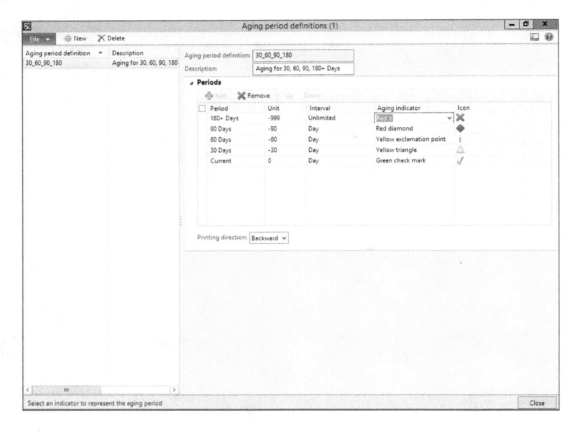

After setting the last final **Aging Indicator** you are done and can click on the **Close** button to exit from the form.

Configuring Account Receivable Collection Parameters

Now that we have configured our aging definitions you can make a small tweak to the **Accounts Receivable** parameters to make it your default aging definition.

Configuring Account Receivable Collection Parameters

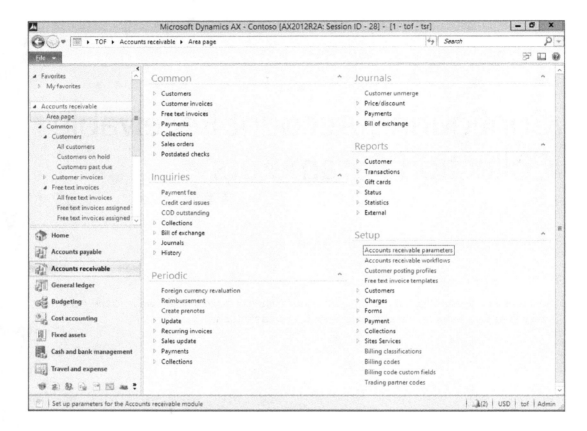

To do this, click on the **Accounts Receivable Parameters** menu item within the **Setup** group of the **Accounts Receivable** area page.

Configuring Account Receivable Collection Parameters

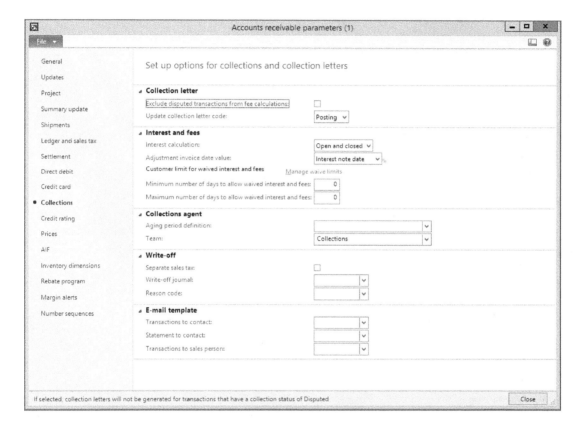

When the **Accounts Receivable Parameters** maintenance form is displayed, select the **Collections** page on the left of the form.

Configuring Account Receivable Collection Parameters

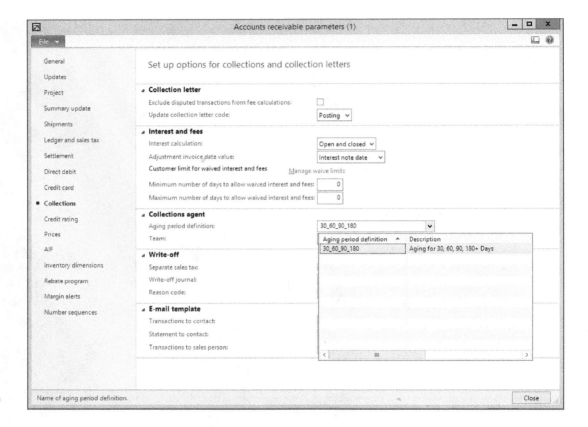

From within the **Collection Agent** tab group, select your new **Aging Period Definition** that you just created from the dropdown list.

Configuring Account Receivable Collection Parameters

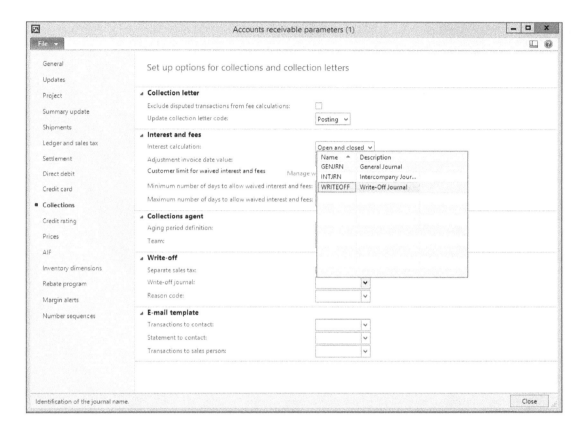

While we are here, we can also link our **WRITEOFF** journal that we created earlier on to the Collections screens by selecting it from the **Write-Off Journal** dropdown list.

Configuring Account Receivable Collection Parameters

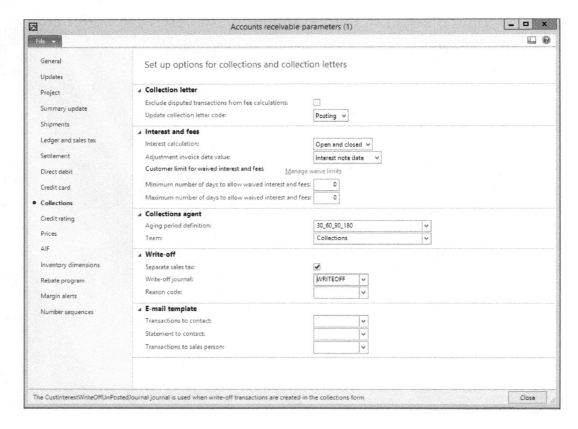

After you have made those quick changes, you can exit the form by clicking on the **Close** button.

Creating an Aging Snapshot

Now that we have our aging definitions configured, we can create an Aging Snapshot which will process all of the customers and create their own aging records for us within the system.

Creating an Aging Snapshot

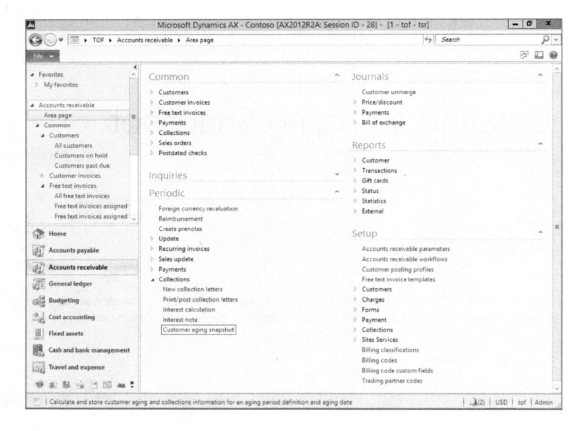

To do this, just click on the **Customer Aging Snapshot** menu item within the **Collections** folder of the **Periodic** group within the **Accounts Receivable** area page.

Creating an Aging Snapshot

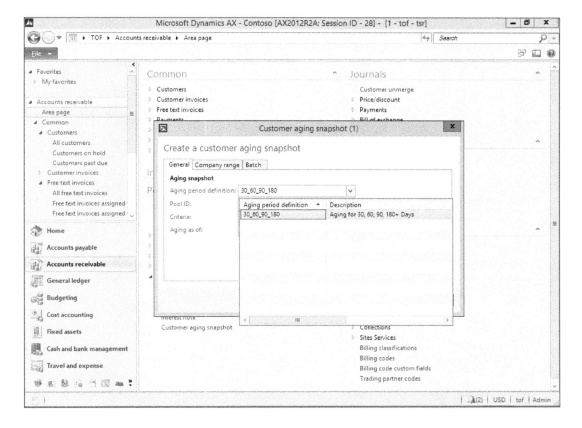

When the **Customer Aging Snapshot** dialog box is displayed, select the **Aging Period Definition** that we just created from the dropdown list.

Creating an Aging Snapshot

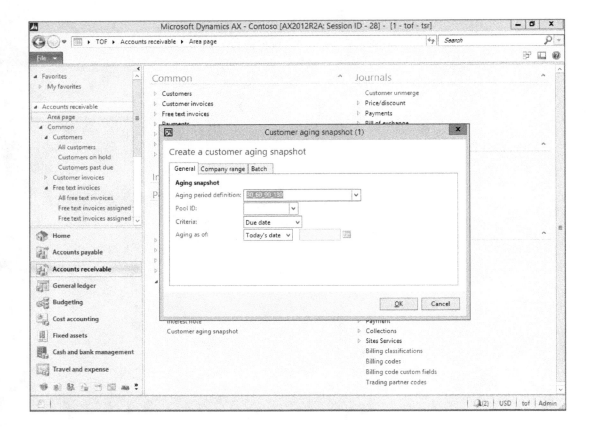

Then click on the **OK** button to create the snapshot.

Creating an Aging Snapshot

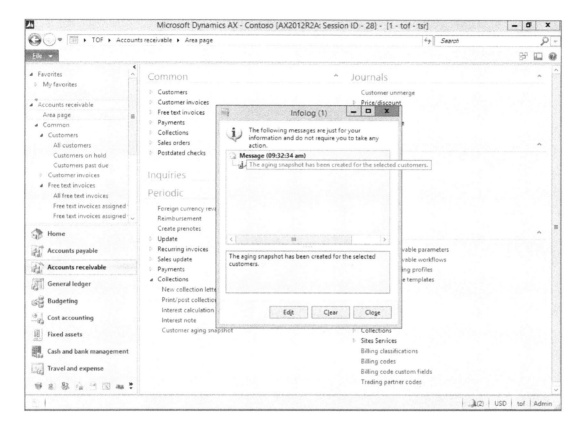

After the snapshot is created you should receive a InfoLog confirming that the process has completed and you are done.

Viewing Collection Statuses Through The Collections Workbench

Now we can start looking at our collections, and there is a workbench that has been designed especially for the collections agent to use to view all of the customer details in one place.

Viewing Collection Statuses Through The Collections Workbench

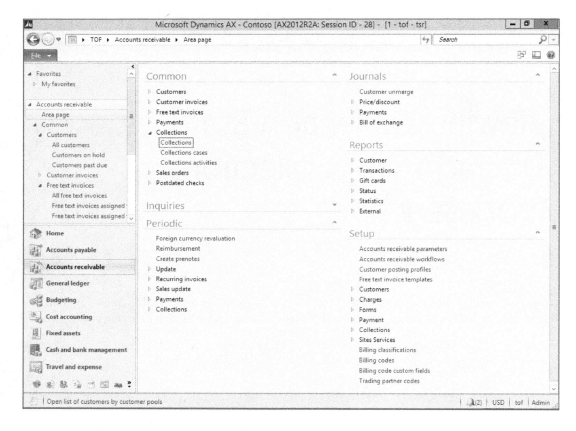

To access the Collections Workbench, click on the **Collections** menu item within the **Collections** folder of the **Common** group of the **Accounts Receivable** area page.

Viewing Collection Statuses Through The Collections Workbench

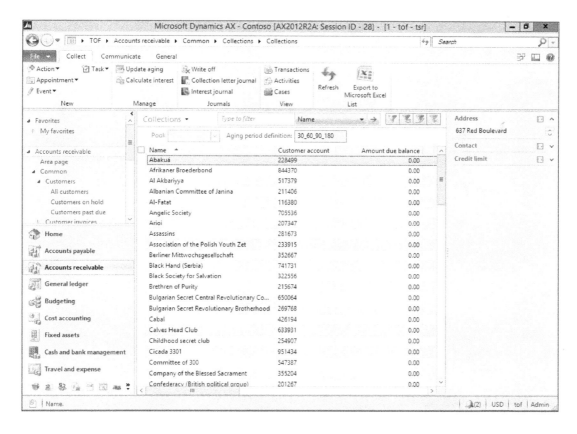

When the **Collections** workbench is displayed you will see all of your customers are listed out and also all of the aging buckets are shown as columns.

Viewing Collection Statuses Through The Collections Workbench

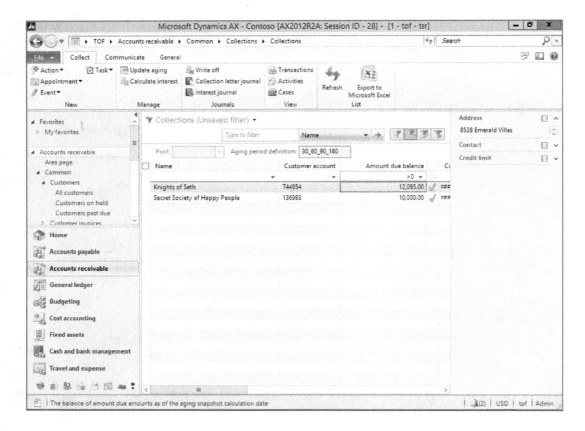

If you want to quickly filter out the view to just the customers that owe money then you can turn on the filter grid by pressing **CTRL+G** and adding a **>0** filter to the **Amount Due Balance** field.

Configuring Customer Collection Pools

Another way that you can filter out your customers though is to create **Collection Pools**. These are predefined filters that you can use to segregate the customers into collection groups by name, or even filter out all of the customers just to the high risk customers that owe too much money.

In this section we will show how to set up a couple different variations of the **Collection Pools**.

Configuring Customer Collection Pools

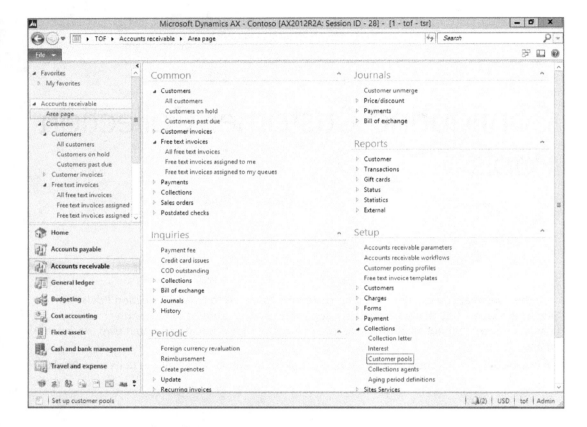

To start off, click on the **Collection Pools** menu item within the **Collections** folder of the **Setup** group within the **Accounts Receivable** area page.

Configuring Customer Collection Pools

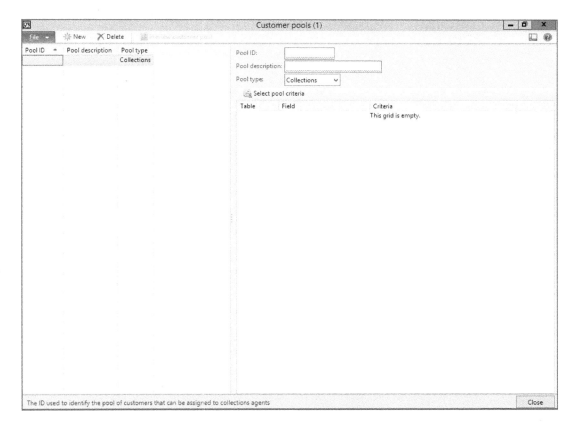

When the **Customer Pools** maintenance form is displayed, click on the **New** button in the menu bar to create a new record.

Configuring Customer Collection Pools

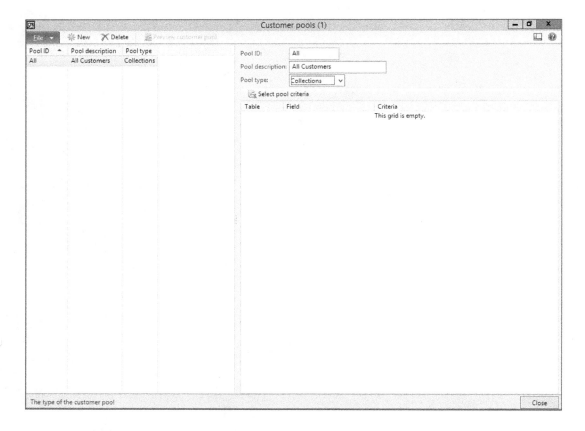

The first pool that we will create will be for all customers, so set the **Pool ID** to **ALL** and the **Pool Description** to **All Customers**.

Then click on the **Select Pool Criteria** button to define the section criteria.

Configuring Customer Collection Pools

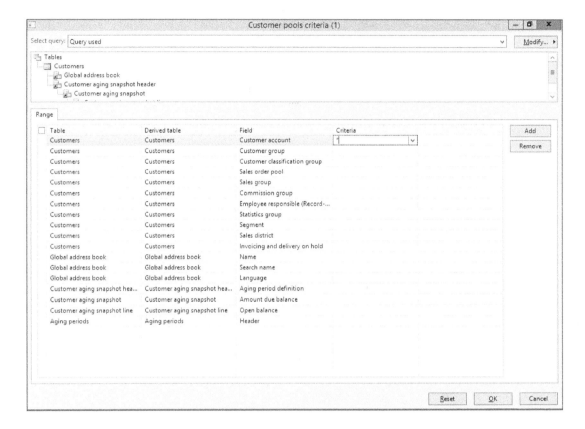

This will open up a criteria builder with all of the common fields that you will want to filter on. For this example, just put a * in the **Customer Account** criteria to select all customers and then click on the **OK** button.

Configuring Customer Collection Pools

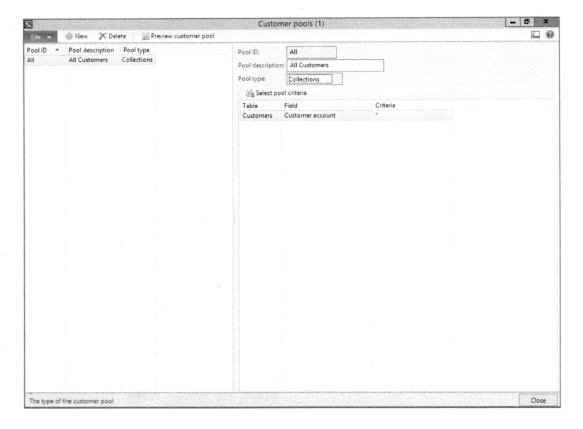

When you return to the **Customer Pools** form you will see that the simple selection has been added to the criteria list.

Configuring Customer Collection Pools

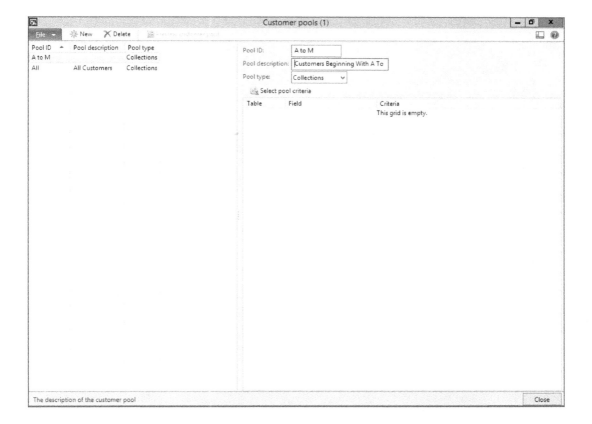

Now we will create a pool for all the customers with names from A to M. To do this click on the **New** button within the menu bar to create a new record, set the **Pool ID** to **A to M**, and the **Pool Description** to **Customers Beginning With A To M**.

Then click on the **Select Pool Criteria** menu button.

Configuring Customer Collection Pools

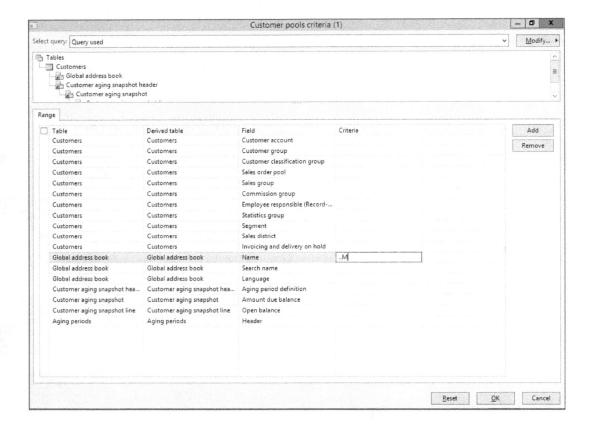

This time when the criteria editor is displayed, set the criteria for the **Name** to **..M**. This is shorthand to say everything up to and including M.

Then click on the **OK** to save the search.

Configuring Customer Collection Pools

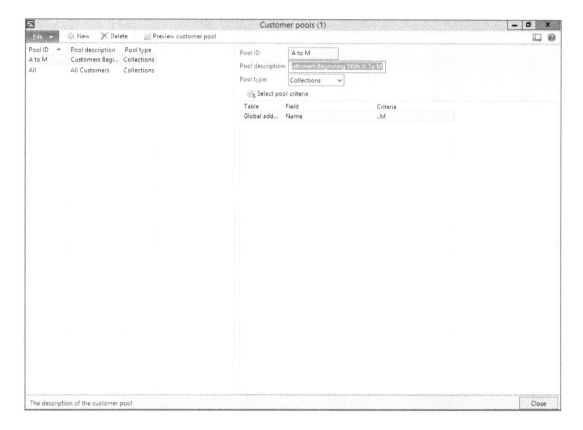

This criteria will have a slightly different selection critera from the first.

Configuring Customer Collection Pools

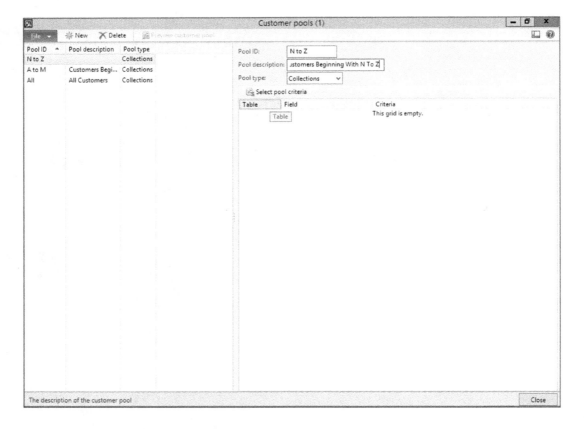

Since we have all the customers from A to M we need to create another corresponding pool for all the customers with names from N to Z. To do this click on the **New** button within the menu bar to create a new record, set the **Pool ID** to **N to Z**, and the **Pool Description** to **Customers Beginning With N To Z**.

Then click on the **Select Pool Criteria** menu button.

Configuring Customer Collection Pools

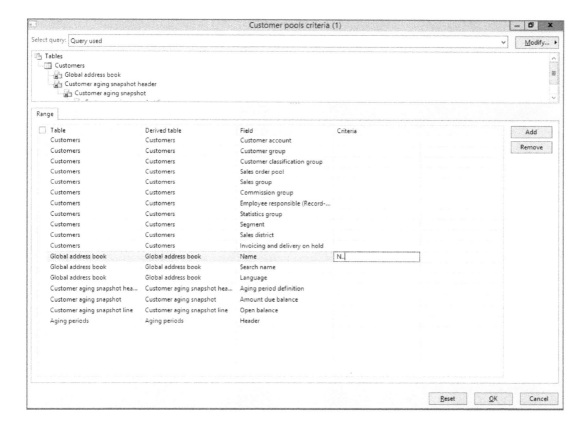

For this one set the **Name** criteria to **N..** And click on the **OK** button.

Configuring Customer Collection Pools

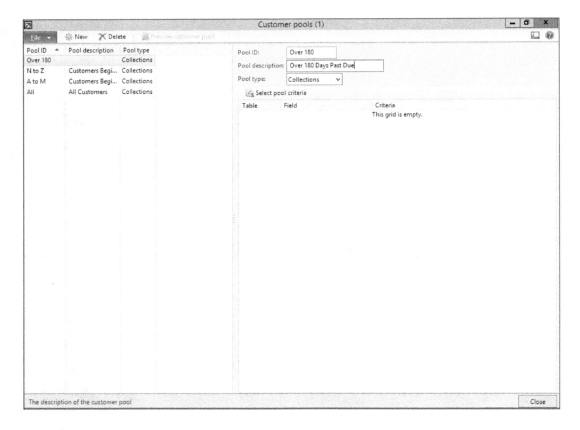

The final **Customer Pool** example that we will create is a little more advanced, because we will want to filter so that we only see customers with past due invoices over 180 days. To do this click on the **New** button within the menu bar to create a new record, set the **Pool ID** to **Over 180**, and the **Pool Description** to **Over 180 Days Past Due**.

Then click on the **Select Pool Criteria** menu button.

Configuring Customer Collection Pools

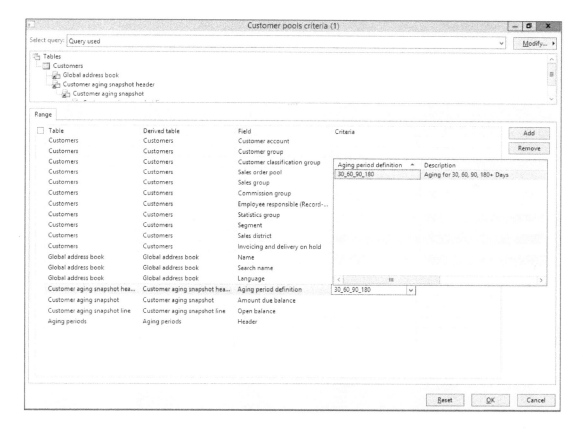

Set the **Aging Period Definition** to the **30_60_90_180** period definition that we created earlier.

Configuring Customer Collection Pools

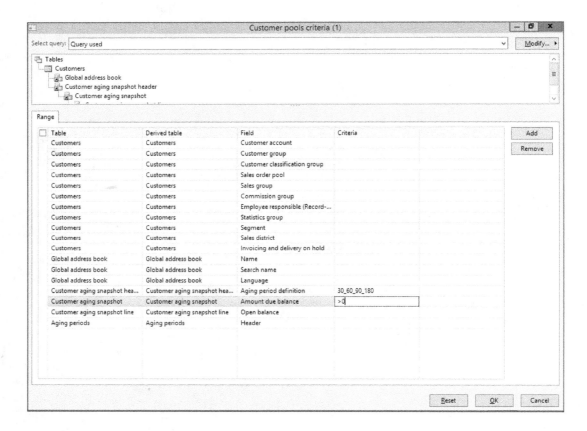

Then set the **Amount Due Balance** criteria to **>0** so that we see only the customers that owe money.

Configuring Customer Collection Pools

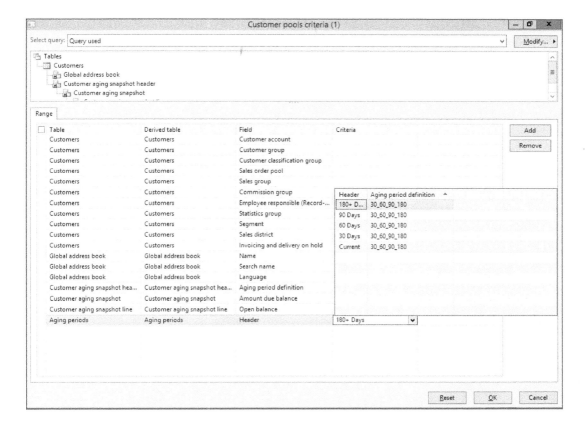

Then set the **Header** criteria to **180+ Days** to filter the transactions to just the 180 day aging column.

Configuring Customer Collection Pools

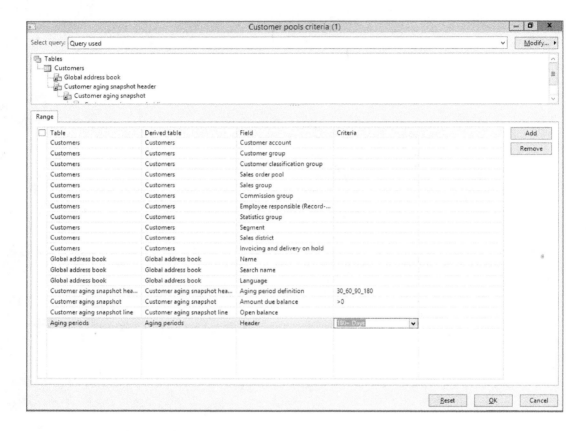

After you have done that, click on the **OK** button to save the criteria and exit from the form.

Configuring Customer Collection Pools

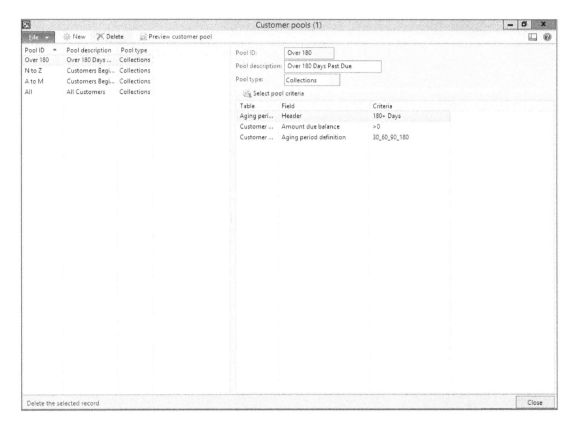

Now you have a few **Customer Pools** defined just click on the **Close** button to exit from the form.

Viewing Collection Statuses By Customer Pool

Now that you have your pools defined you can use them within the collection workbench.

Viewing Collection Statuses By Customer Pool

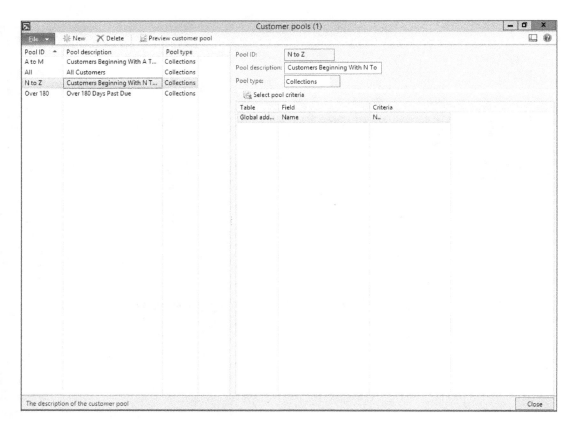

A quick trick to viewing the customer pool is to open up the **Customer Pools** maintenance form, select the pool that you want to view and click on the **Preview Customer Pool** item in the menu bar.

Viewing Collection Statuses By Customer Pool

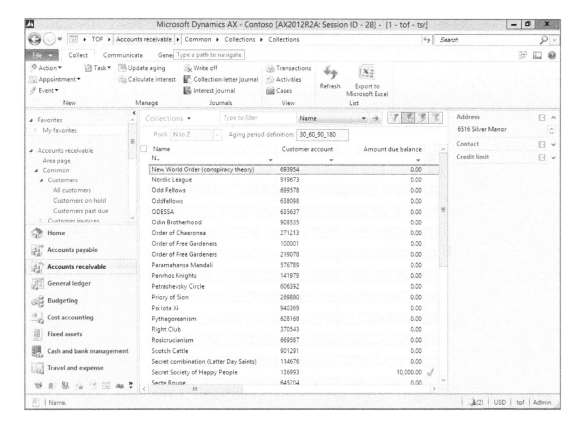

This will take you straight to the **Collections** workbench and will filter out the records to match the pool.

How easy is that?

Configuring Collection Letters

Another collection mechanism that you may want to configure are the Collection Letters. These allow you to create different escalation paths for collections that you can use for different customer groups that have differing levels of severity and also automatic charges applied to the customer account.

Configuring Collection Letters

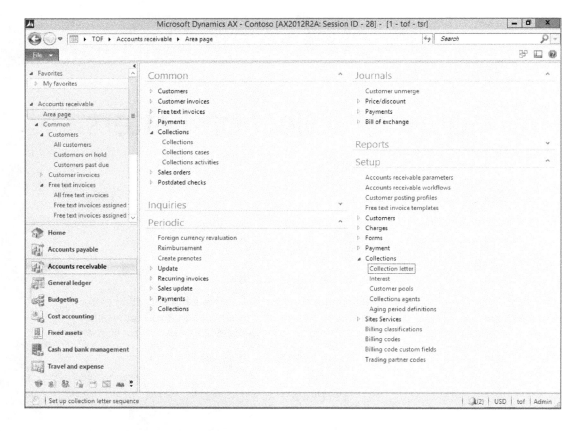

To do this, click on the **Collection Letter** menu item within the **Collections** folder of the **Setup** group of the **Accounts Receivable** area page.

Configuring Collection Letters

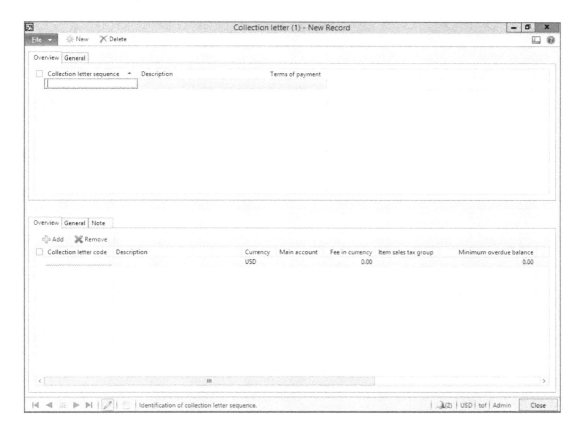

When the **Collection Letter** maintenance form is displayed, click on the **New** button in the menu bar to create a new record.

Configuring Collection Letters

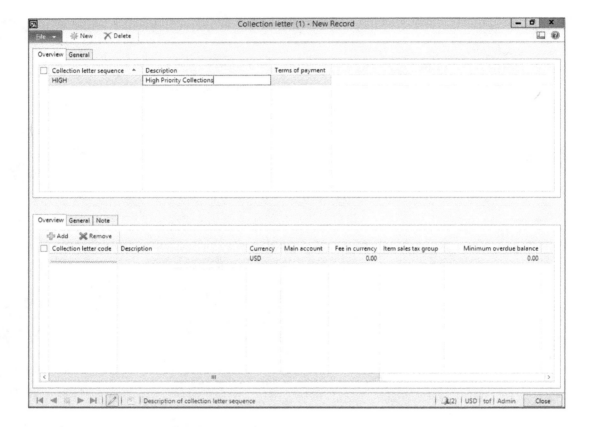

Set the **Collection Letter Sequence** field to **HIGH** and the **Description** to **High Priority Collections.**

Configuring Collection Letters

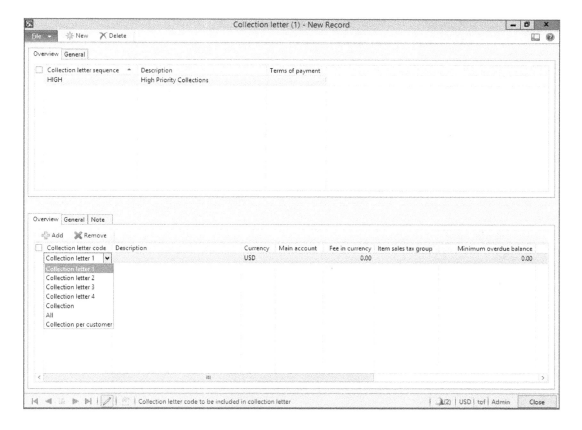

Then from within the **Overview** tab in the lower half of the form, click on the **Add** button to add a new collection letter stage and select the **Collection Letter 1** value from the **Collection Letter Code** field. These will indicate the type of letter that will be sent to the customer. As the collections extend you can guess that the wording will become slightly different.

Configuring Collection Letters

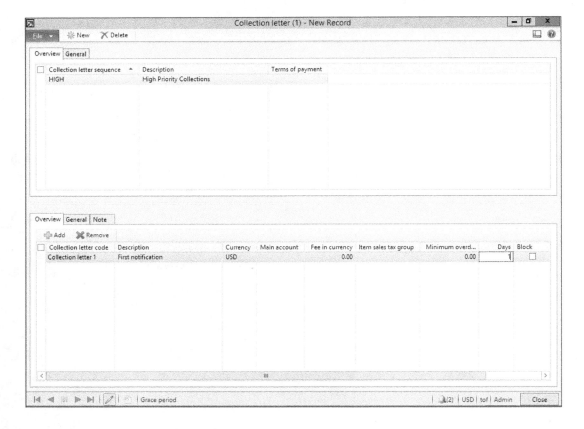

Set the **Description** to **First Notification** and then set the **Days** to 1 for the first notice.

Configuring Collection Letters

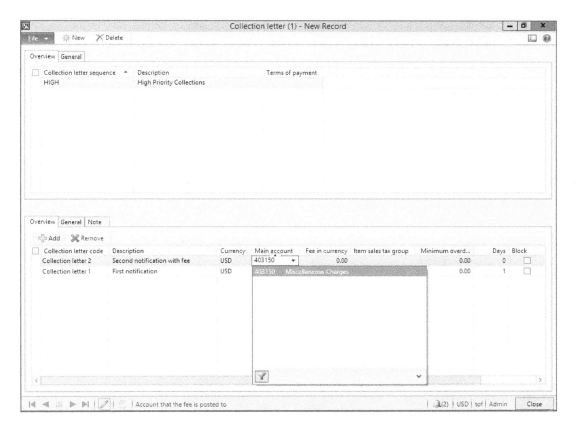

Now click on the **Add** button again to add the next notification. This time set the **Collection Letter Code** to **Collection Letter 2**.

For this collection letter we will be assessing a fee for the account being delinquent, to select a **Main Account** that you will be posting the charge to from the dropdown list.

Configuring Collection Letters

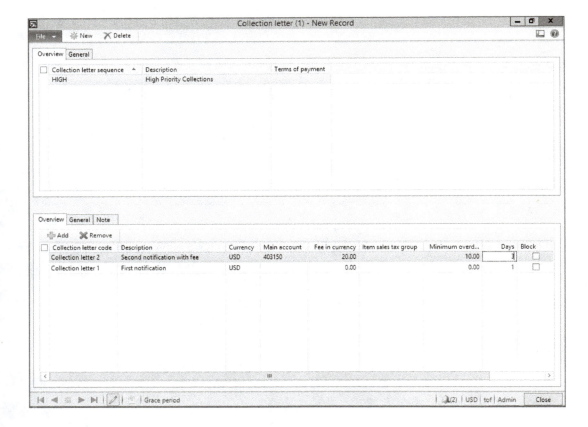

Then set the **Fee In Currency** for the charge to **20**.

Set the **Minimum Overdue** amount to be **10** so that we don't charge customers fees for small amounts overdue.

And then set the **Days** to **3** so that we have a little bit of an interval between the first and second collection letter.

Configuring Collection Letters

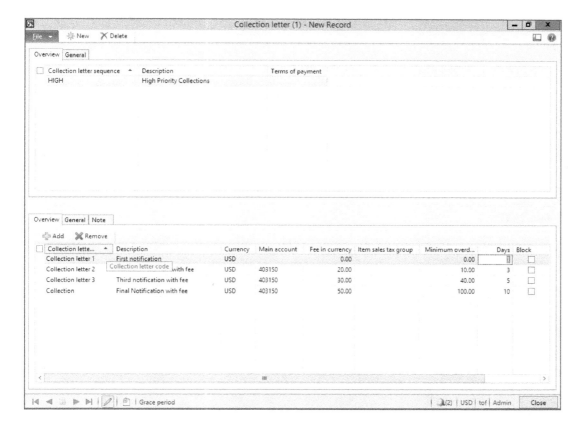

Keep on adding additional lines for the collection statuses, finishing with the **Collection Letter Code** of **Collection** for the most severe collection notice.

Configuring Collection Letters

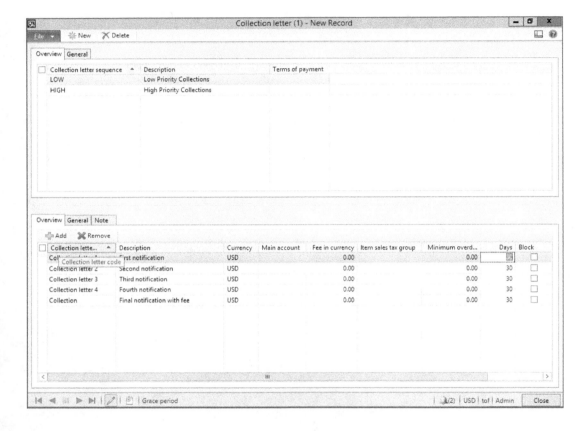

You can create additional **Collection Letters** as well that don't necessarily have service charges associated with them.

When you are done, click on the **Close** button to exit from the form.

Printing Customer Statements From The Collections Workbench

The Collections Workbench is not just for viewing the customer aging's, it is also the one stop shop for the collections agents to interact with the customers. One example of this is that they can create all manner of document for the customer including statements.

Printing Customer Statements From The Collections Workbench

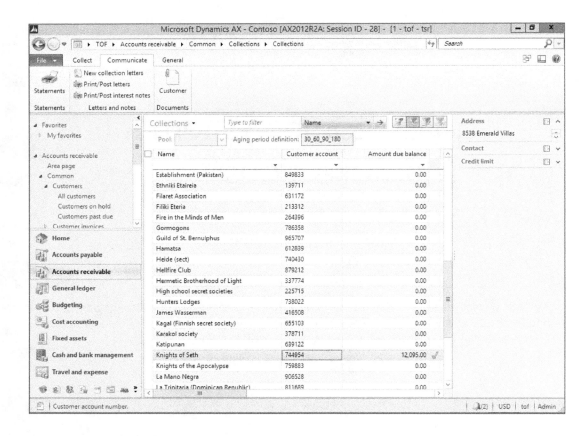

To do this, open up the **Collections Workbench** and select the customer that you need to send the statement to. Then click on the **Statements** button within the **Statements** group of the **Communicate** ribbon bar.

Printing Customer Statements From The Collections Workbench

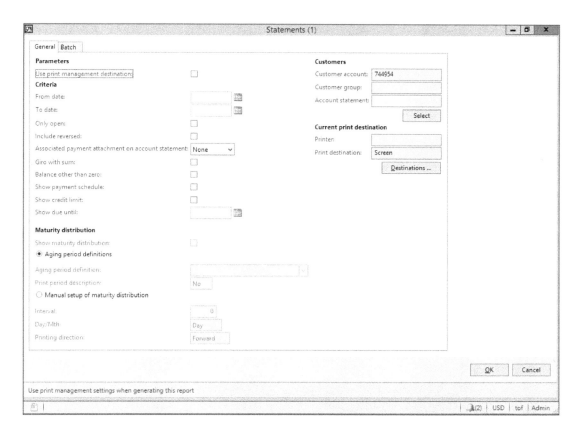

When the **Statements** selection dialog is displayed, you can select from a number of different options for the statement, but to make this simple, just click on the **OK** button to take the defaults.

Printing Customer Statements From The Collections Workbench

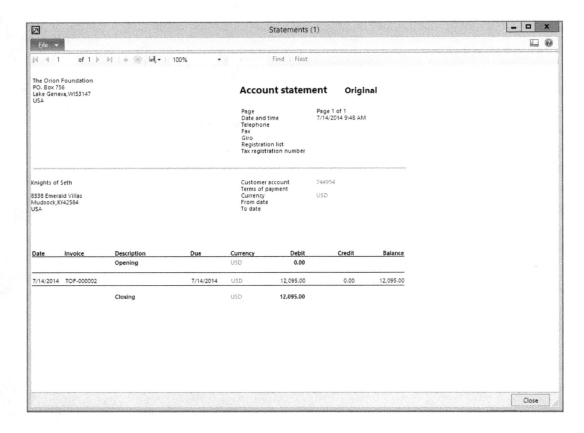

In a couple of seconds you will have your Customer Statement.

CONFIGURING CASH RECEIPTS

Hopefully you won't have to use the **Collections Workbench** very much and your customers will just pay their invoices on time, or before they are due. So the next area that we are going to look at is the **Cash Receipts** functions within Dynamics AX and show you how to record customer payments.

Creating a Payment Journal

All cash receipts are done within Dynamics AX through **Payment Journals**. These can be used to receive individual or batches of payments.

Creating a Payment Journal

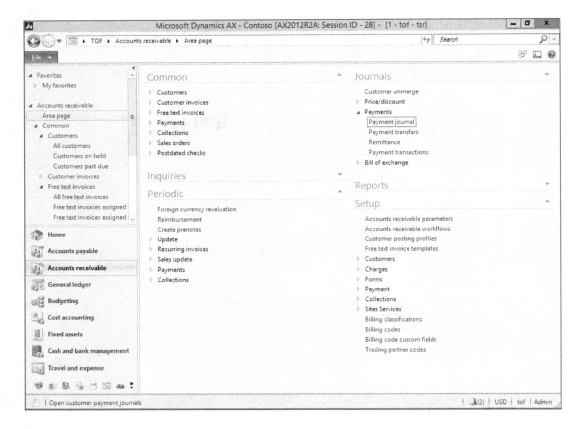

To enter a **Cash Receipt** click on the **Payment Journal** menu item within the **Payments** folder of the **Journals** group of the **Accounts Receivable** area page.

Creating a Payment Journal

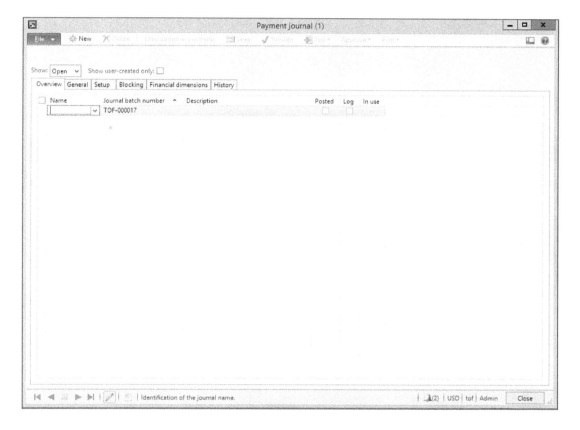

When the **Payment Journal** maintenance form is displayed, click on the **New** button within the menu bar to create a new record.

Creating a Payment Journal

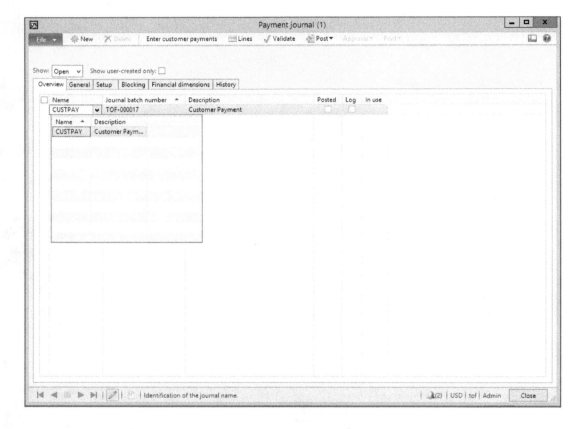

Then from the **Name** dropdown list select your **CUSTPAY** journal that you created earlier on.

Tip: If you want to segregate our different receipts then you can create additional Payment Journal types.

Creating a Payment Journal

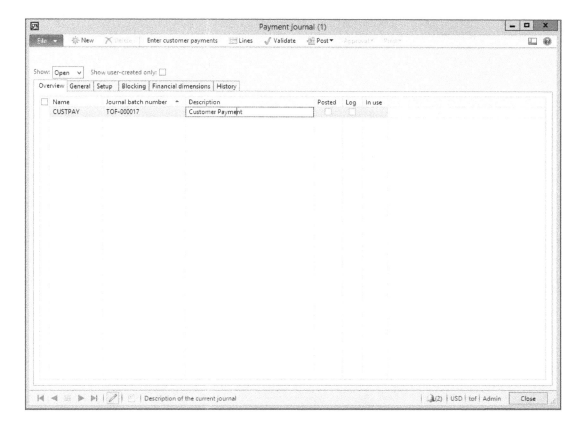

If you want to can add a different description for the Payment Journal for reference.

But to enter the payments, click on the **Enter Customer Payments** button in the menu bar.

Creating a Payment Journal

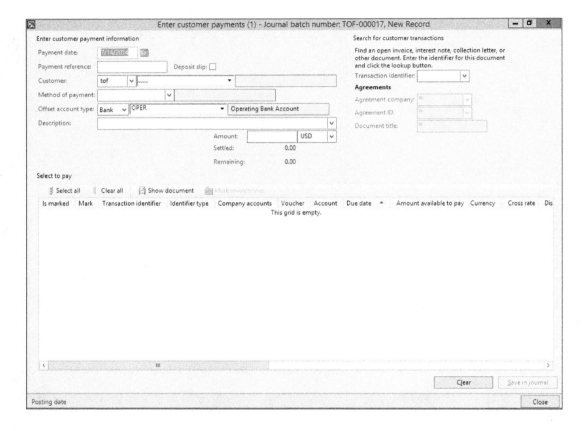

This will open up the **Customer Payment** entry form.

Creating a Payment Journal

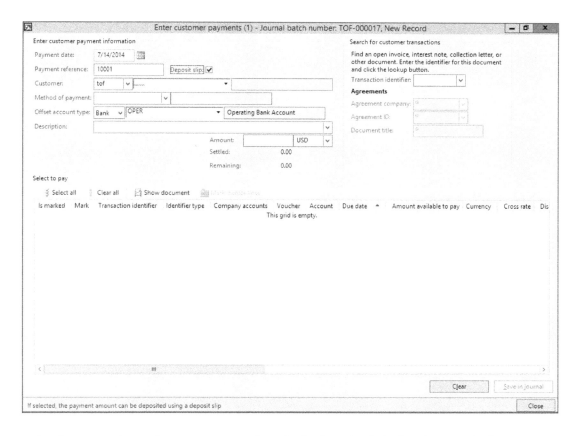

Tip: If you want Dynamics AX to create a deposit slip then check the handy **Deposit Slip** checkbox.

Creating a Payment Journal

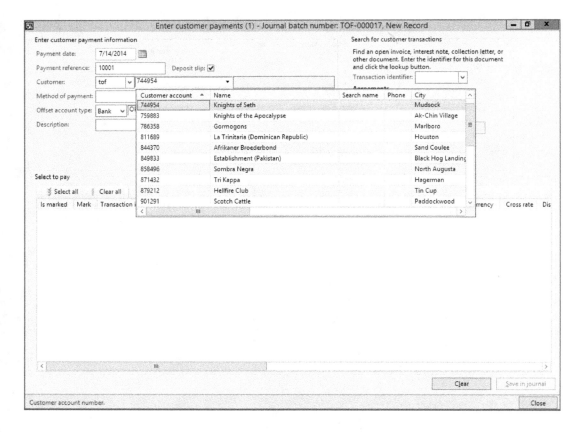

Now select the **Customer** from the dropdown list that you are entering the payment for.

Creating a Payment Journal

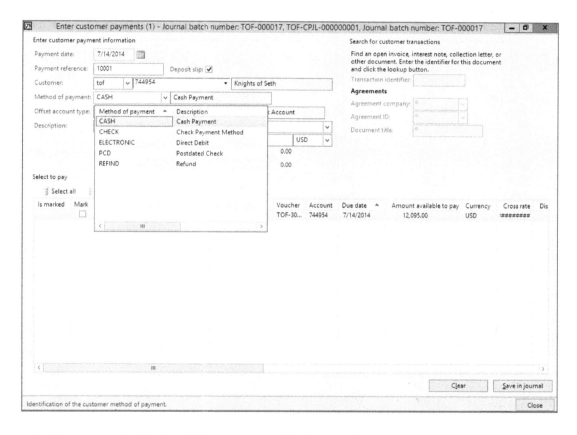

And then select the **Method Of Payment** that is being used by the customer from the dropdown list.

Creating a Payment Journal

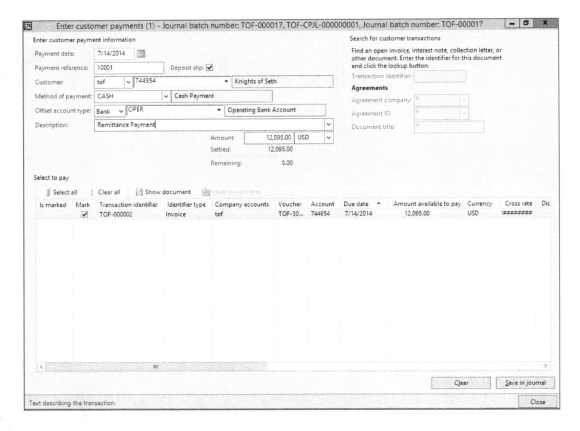

Notice that this will automatically default in the Bank Account information for you from the Method Of Payment.

Within the bottom half of the form you will also see all of the invoices that are open for the customer. If they are paying the invoice in full, then all you need to do is click on the **Mark** checkbox against the appropriate invoice.

Then to add the payment to the journal, click on the **Save In Journal** button.

Creating a Payment Journal

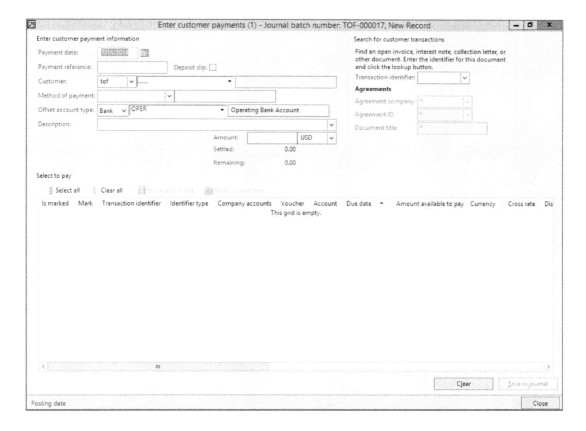

The form will then reset and you can move onto the next payment in the batch.

When you have finished entering in your cash receipts, just click on the **Close** button to exit from the form.

Creating a Payment Journal

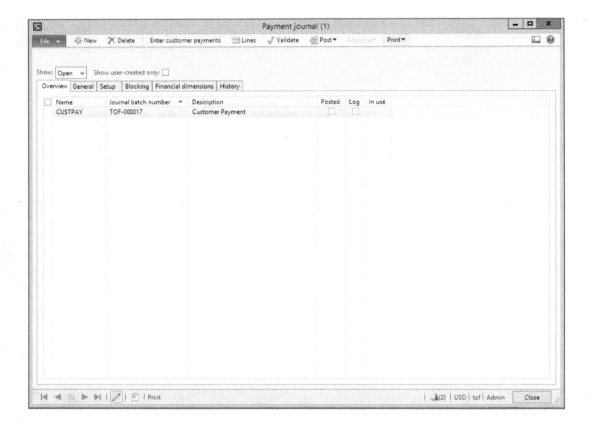

This will return you back to the **Payment Journal** maintenance form.

If you want to see the customer payment details, then click on the **Lines** button in the menu bar.

Creating a Payment Journal

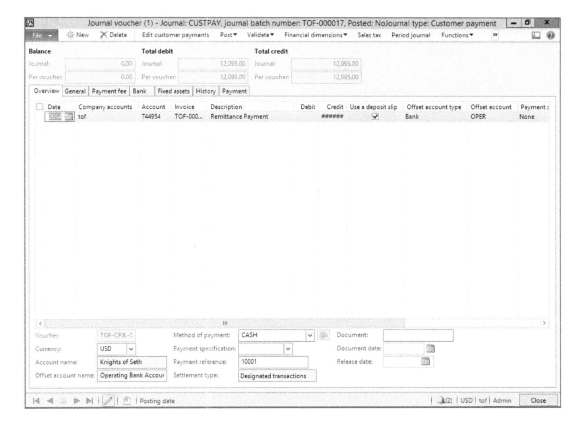

This will take you into the full receipts batch with all of the receipts.

Creating a Payment Journal

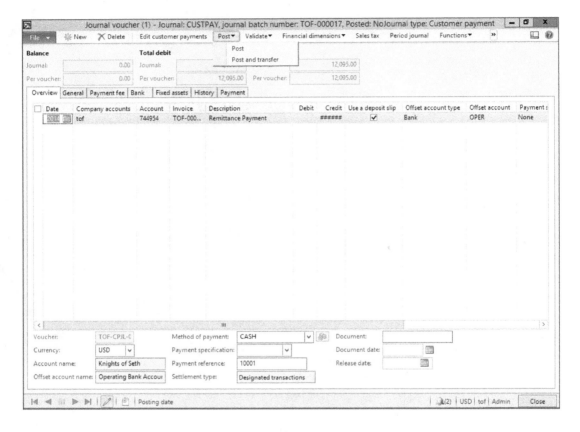

To post and update the cash receipts, click on the **Post** button in the menu bar and select the **Post** submenu item.

Creating a Payment Journal

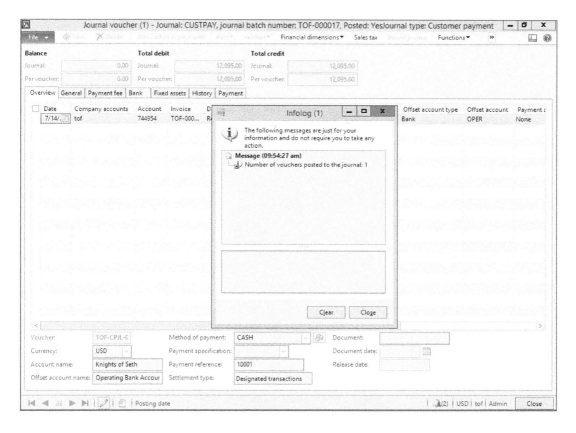

If everything has been entered correctly then you will get a simple InfoLog telling you that the journal was posted.

Creating a Payment Journal

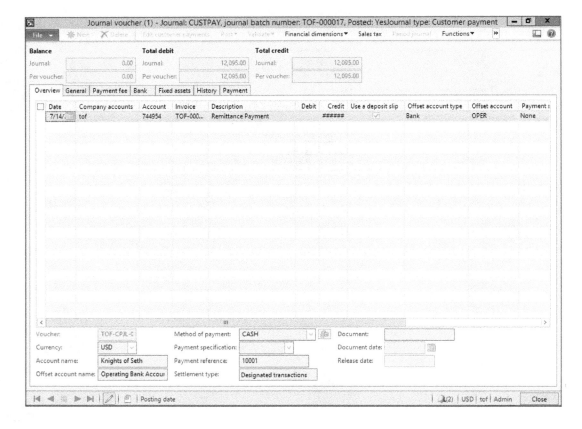

And you will notice that you can no longer make changes to the Payment Journal.

Creating a Payment Journal

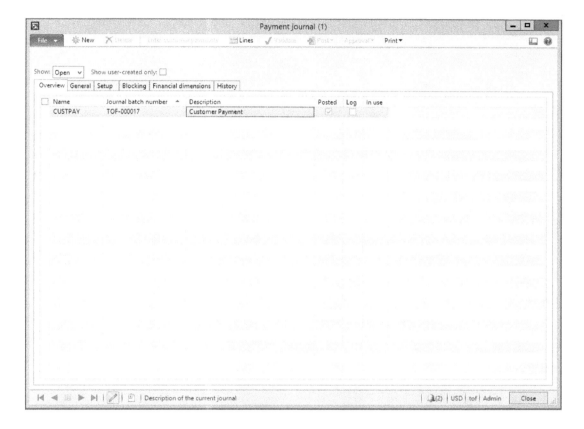

When you return to the **Payment Journal** list page, you will notice that it has been marked as **Posted** there as well.

Creating a Payment Journal

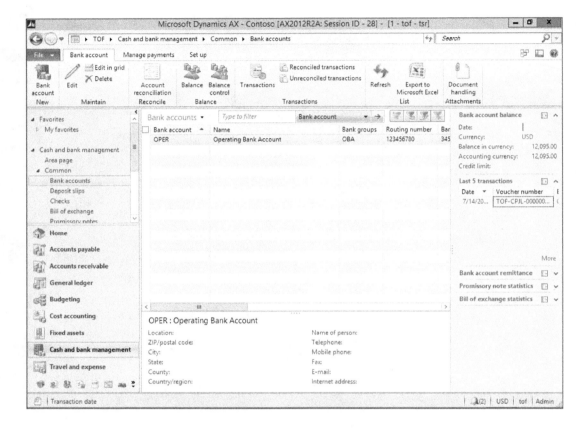

Just to make sure you can even go to your bank account and you will see that the cash receipt has been applied within there as well.

Now we're cooking with gas!

Manually Updating Customer Aging's Through The Collections Dashboard

As a side note, because the Collections Workbench is linked to the aging's snapshot that you ran earlier. You don't have to run that process though if you just want to refresh the customers account information based on a cash receipt being applied. You can do that directly from the **Collections Workbench.**

Manually Updating Customer Aging's Through The Collections Dashboard

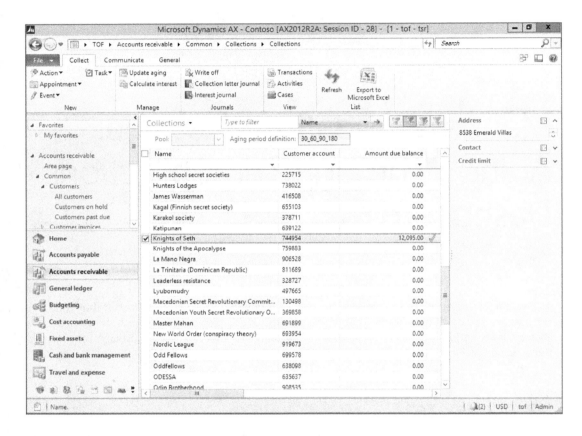

To do this, click on the customer that you want to refresh the aging for and then click on the **Update Aging** button within the **Manage** group of the **Collect** ribbon bar.

Manually Updating Customer Aging's Through The Collections Dashboard

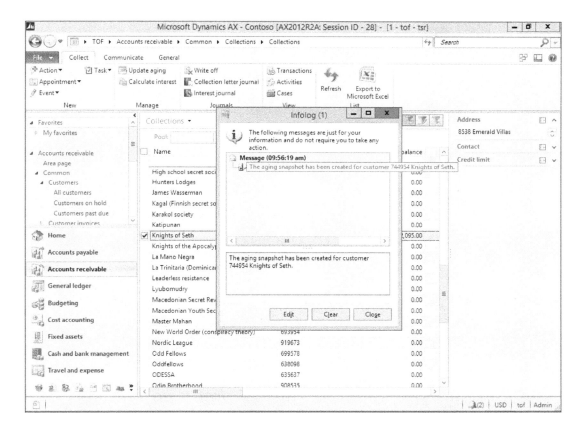

You will get a quick note from Dynamics AX that the aging has been updated.

Manually Updating Customer Aging's Through The Collections Dashboard

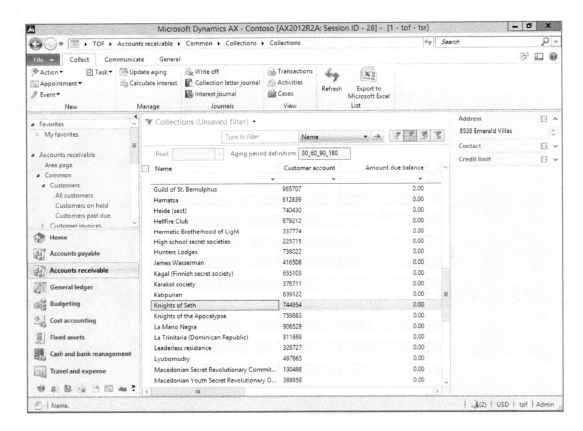

And now when you return to the customer list the balances will be adjusted for that customer.

Cleaning up your collections has never been so easy.

CONFIGURING DEDUCTION MANAGEMENT

Unfortunately customers don't always pay the amount that you ask them to, and tracking the discrepancies can be a chore in itself, because you may have given an incentive to the customer that they are taking as a valid deduction, the customer may be penalizing you for one reason or another, or they may just be wrong. You don't want to have the invoices sitting out there waiting to be investigated and cluttering up the aging's though, which is where the **Deduction Management** feature comes into play. This allows you to record deductions as you are receiving cash and close out the invoices. Then the deductions are set them aside for someone to investigate them and decide if they are valid or not.

In this section we will show how to set up and use the **Deduction Management** features.

Configuring Deduction Journal Types

The first thing that we need to do is to configure a new **Journal Type** for our deductions to be tracked through.

Configuring Deduction Journal Types

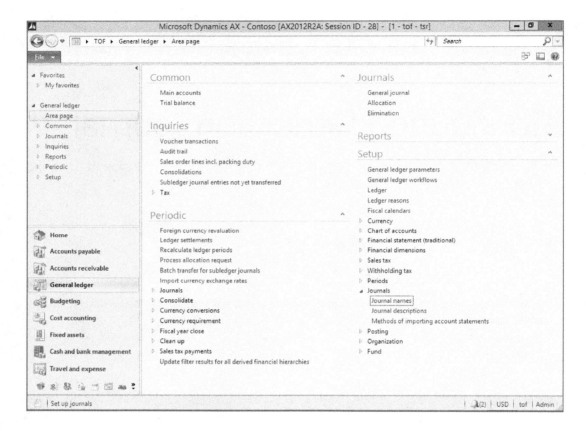

To do this, click on the **Journal Names** menu item within the **Journals** folder of the **Setup** group within the **General Ledger** area page.

Configuring Deduction Journal Types

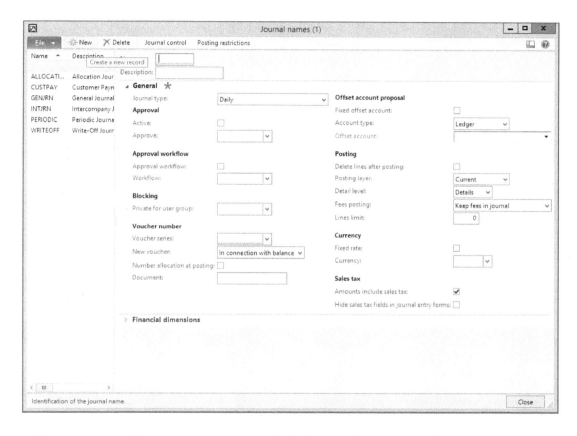

When the **Journal Names** maintenance form is displayed, click on the **New** button in the menu bar to create a new record.

Configuring Deduction Journal Types

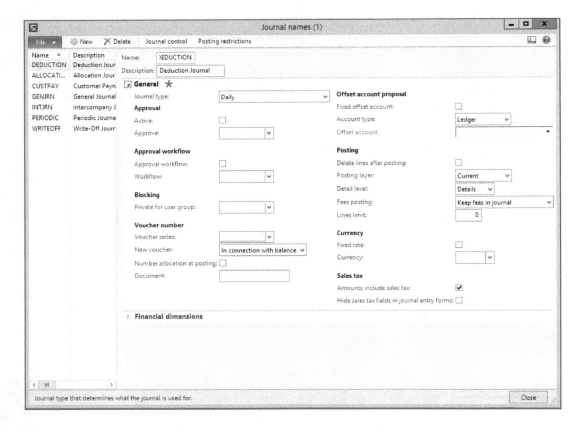

Then set the **Name** to **DEDUCTION** and the **Description** to **Deduction Journal**.

Configuring Deduction Journal Types

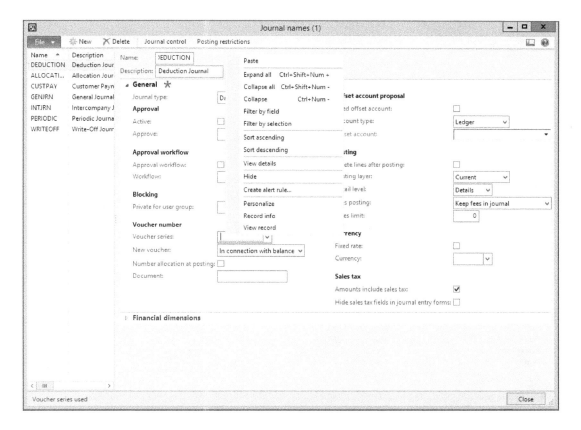

Next we need to create a new number sequence for the deduction journals. To do this, right-mouse-click on the **Voucher Name** field and select the **View Details** menu item.

Configuring Deduction Journal Types

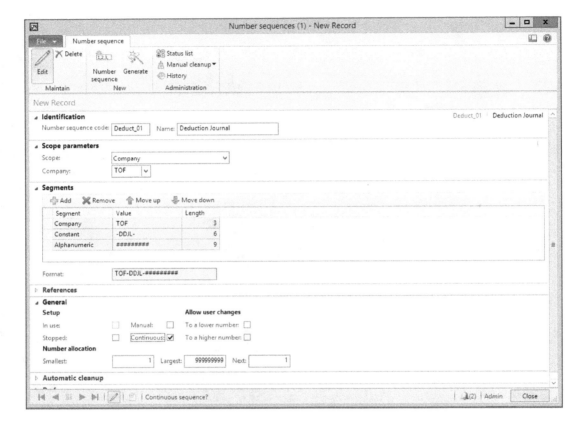

When the **Number Sequences** maintenance form is displayed, click on the **Number Sequence** button within the **New** group of the **Number Sequence** ribbon bar to create a new number sequence.

Set the **Number Sequence Code** to **Deduct_01** and the **Name** to **Deduction Journal**.

Then set the **Scope** to your legal entity, and also format the segment to identify the journal as a deduction.

When you are done, click the **Close** button.

Configuring Deduction Journal Types

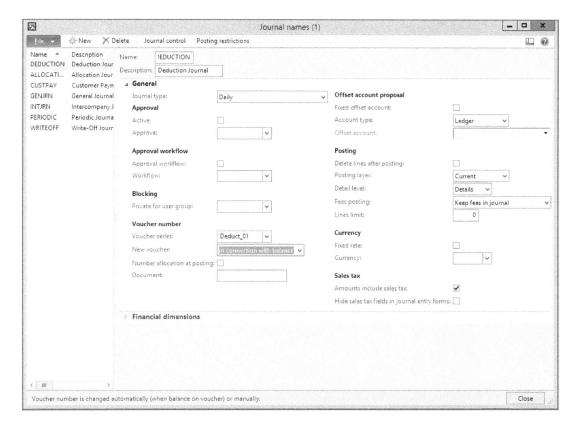

Now when you return to the **Journal Names** form, you can assign your deduction journal the new number sequence and then click on the **Close** button.

Configuring Trade Allowance Management Parameters For Deductions

Now we need to make a couple of tweaks within the **Trade Allowance Management Parameters** to make sure that our deductions work correctly.

Configuring Trade Allowance Management Parameters For Deductions

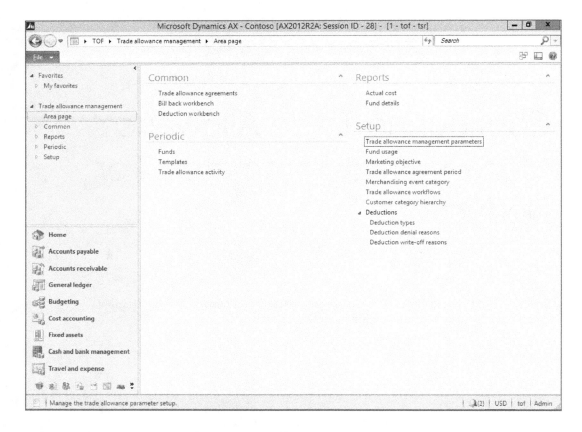

To do this, click on the **Trade Allowance Management Parameters** menu item wiothin the **Setup** group of the **Trade Allowance Management** area page.

Configuring Trade Allowance Management Parameters For Deductions

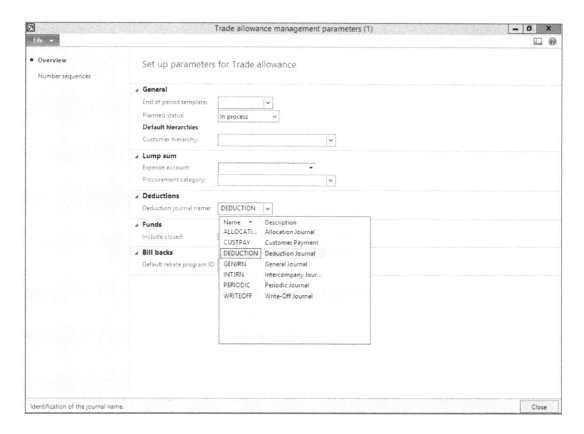

When the **Trade Allowance Management Parameters** form is displayed, select your **DEDUCTION** journal that you just created from the **Deduction Journal** dropdown list.

All done – now just click the **Close** button.

Configuring Deduction Types

As you are recording your deductions at cash receipt you may want to classify them differently based on information that the customer is passing on to you. So in order to do that we will configure a few **Deduction Types**.

Configuring Deduction Types

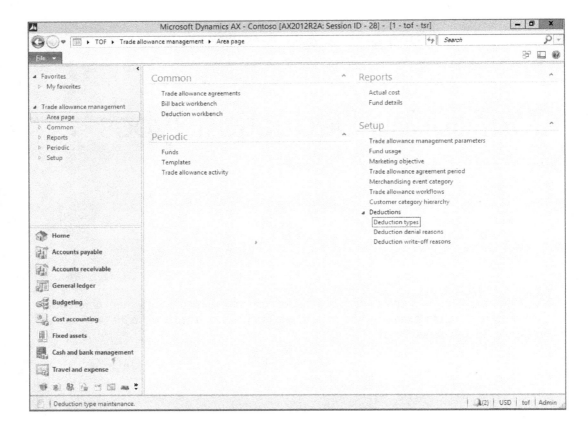

To do this, click on the **Deduction Types** menu item within the **Deductions** folder of the **Setup** group within the **Trade Allowance Management** area page.

Configuring Deduction Types

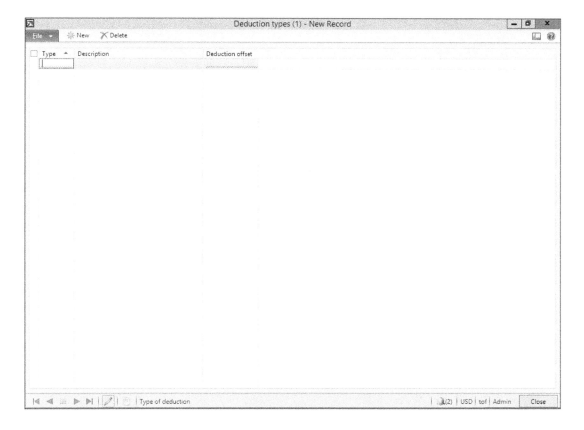

When the **Deduction Types** maintenance form is displayed, click on the **New** button in the menu bar to create a new record.

Configuring Deduction Types

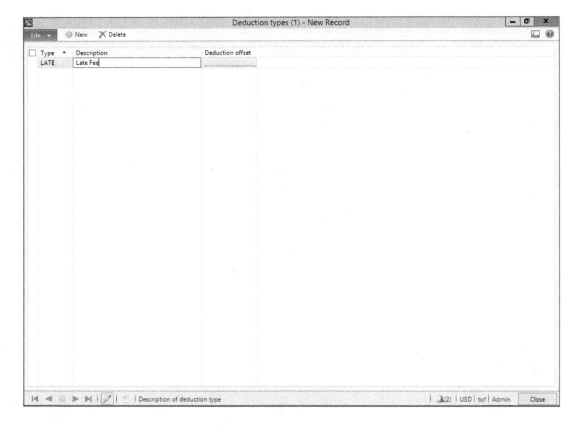

Set the Deduction **Type** and the **Description**.

Configuring Deduction Types

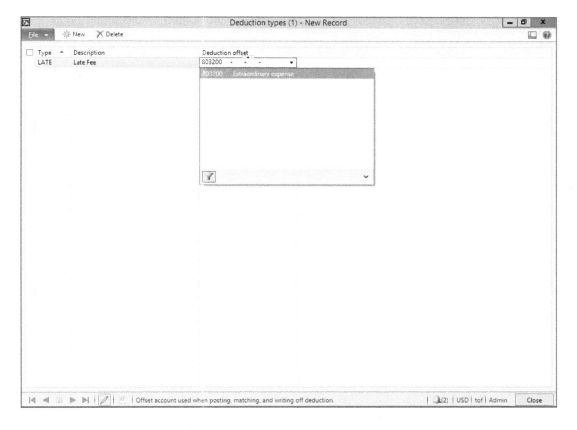

And then from the **Deduction Offset** field, select the main account that you want to post the deduction against.

Configuring Deduction Types

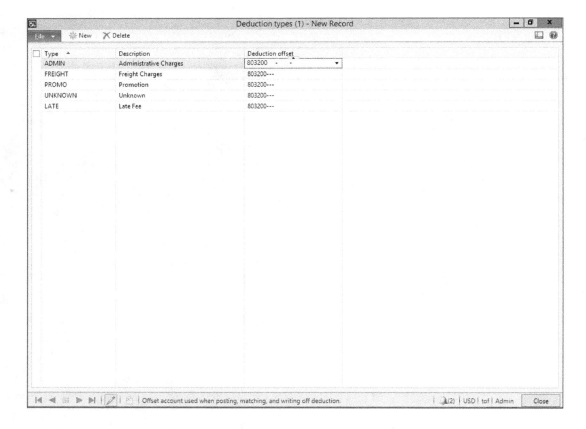

You can continue adding additional **Deduction Types** and then when you are finished, just click on the **Close** button to exit from the form.

Configuring Deduction Denial Reasons

When you are investigating the **Deductions** you have two choices in processing them. You can approve them, or you can deny them. When you deny a deduction you can associate a reason code with the transaction as it's returned to the customer account, so in this step we will configure a couple of **Deduction Denial Reasons**.

Configuring Deduction Denial Reasons

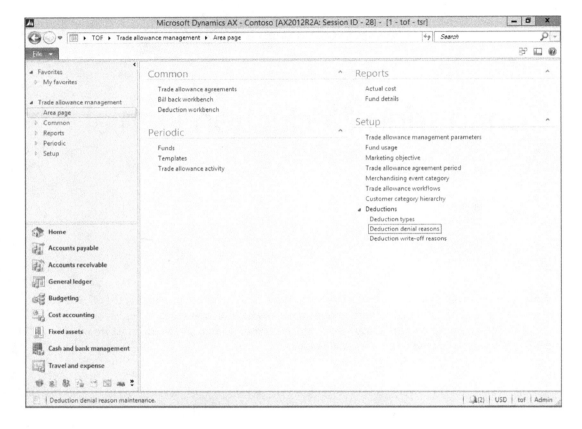

To do this, click on the **Deduction Denial Reasons** menu item within the **Deductions** folder of the **Setup** group of the **Trade Allowance Management** area page.

Configuring Deduction Denial Reasons

When the **Deduction Denial Reasons** maintenance form is displayed, click on the **New** button in the menu bar to create a new record.

Configuring Deduction Denial Reasons

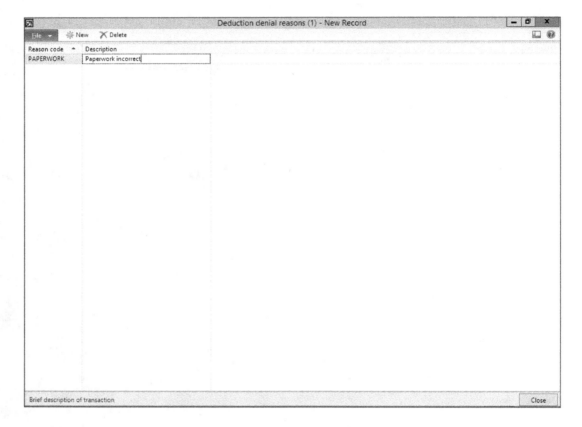

Then assign the record a **Reason Code** and a **Description**.

Configuring Deduction Denial Reasons

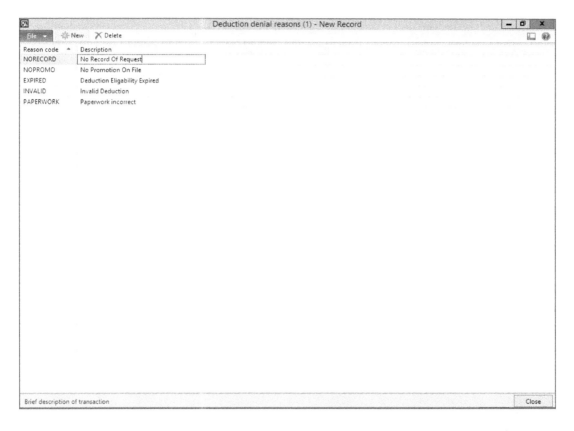

You can continue adding additional **Deduction Denial Reasons** and then when you are finished, just click on the **Close** button to exit from the form.

Configuring Deduction Write Off Codes

If the deduction is valid then you will need to assign it to a **Write-Off** code, so in this step we will configure a few to use later on.

Configuring Deduction Write Off Codes

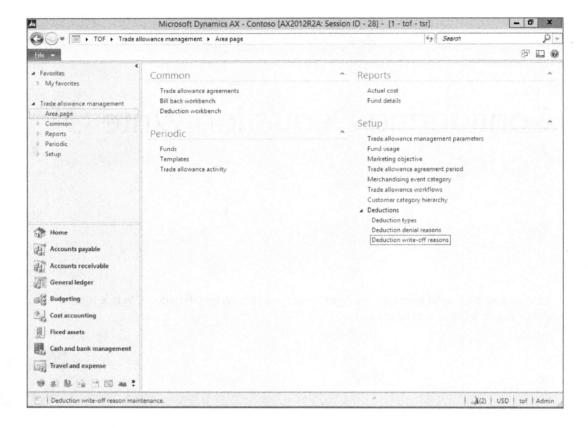

To do this, click on the **Deduction Write-Off Reasons** menu item within the **Deductions** folder of the **Setup** group of the **Trade Allowance Management** area page.

Configuring Deduction Write Off Codes

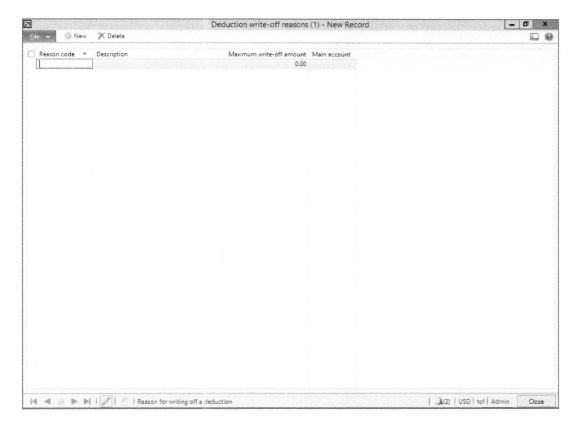

When the **Deduction Write-Off Reasons** maintenance form is displayed, click on the **New** button in the menu bar to create a new record.

Configuring Deduction Write Off Codes

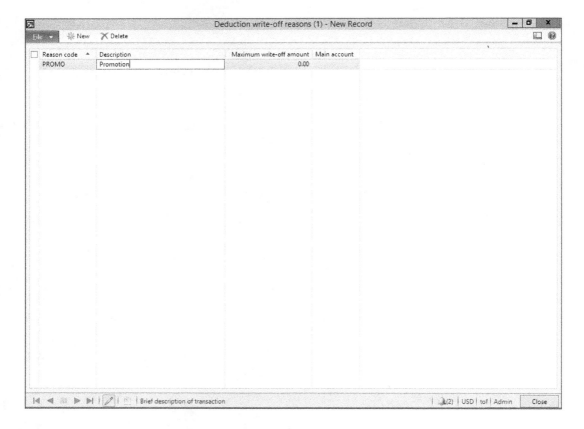

Then assign the record a **Reason Code** and a **Description**.

Configuring Deduction Write Off Codes

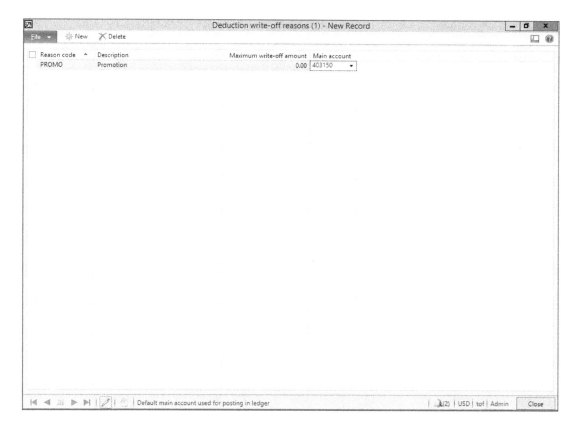

Then assign a **Main Account** that you want to post the write-off amount to within the ledger.

Configuring Deduction Write Off Codes

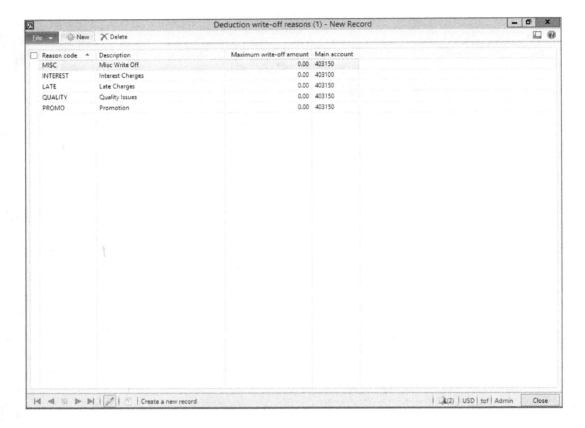

You can continue adding additional **Deduction Write-Off Reasons** and then when you are finished, just click on the **Close** button to exit from the form.

Entering Customer Payments With Deductions

Now that we have our codes and controls configured for **Deduction Management** we can test it out by entering a Deduction within the Payment Journal entry process.

Entering Customer Payments With Deductions

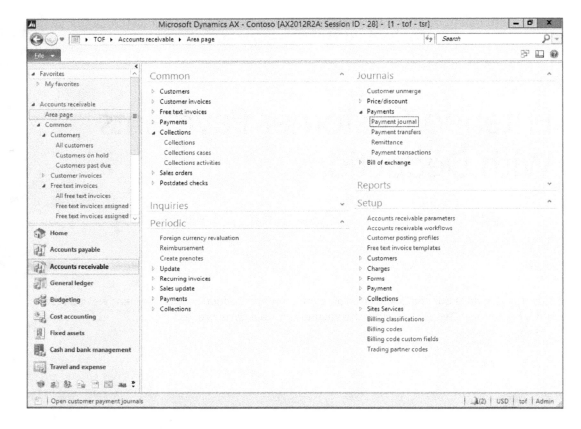

To do this, click on the **Payment Journal** menu item within the **Payments** folder of the **Journals** group of the **Accounts Receivable** area page.

Entering Customer Payments With Deductions

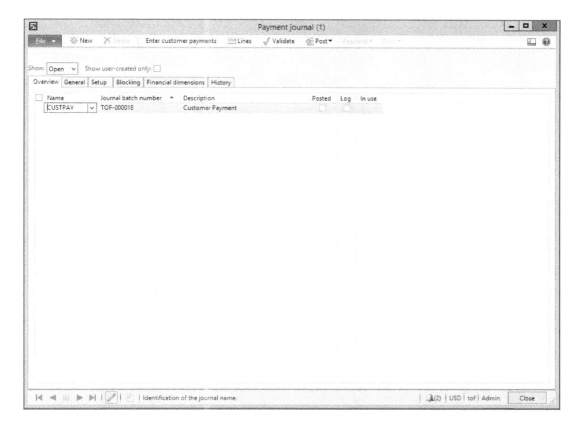

When the **Payment Journal** maintenance form is displayed, click on the **New** button within the menu bar to create a new record, select the **CUSTPAY** Journal Type and then click on the **Enter Customer Payments** button within the menu bar.

Entering Customer Payments With Deductions

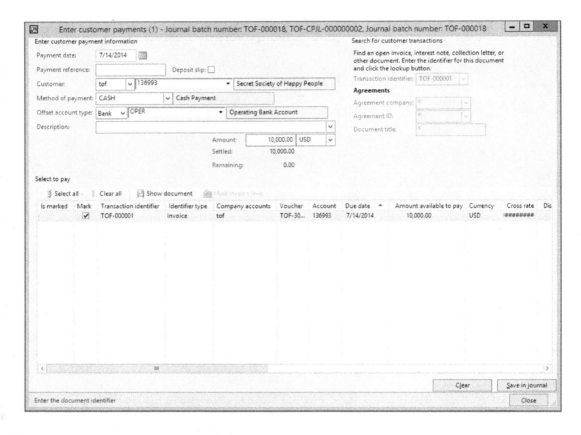

Enter in the **Customer Payment** details and click the **Save In Journal** and then the **Close** button.

Entering Customer Payments With Deductions

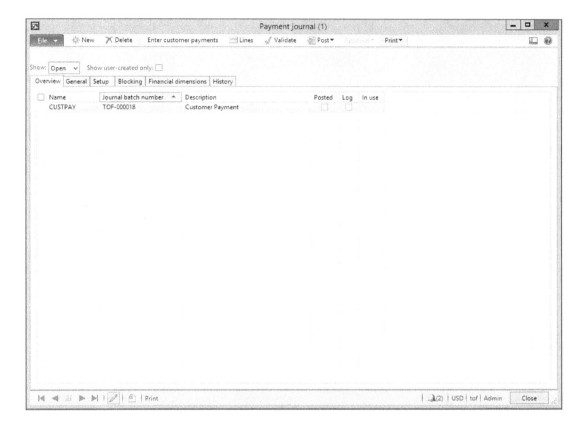

When you return to the **Payment Journal** form, click on the **Lines** button in the menu bar.

Entering Customer Payments With Deductions

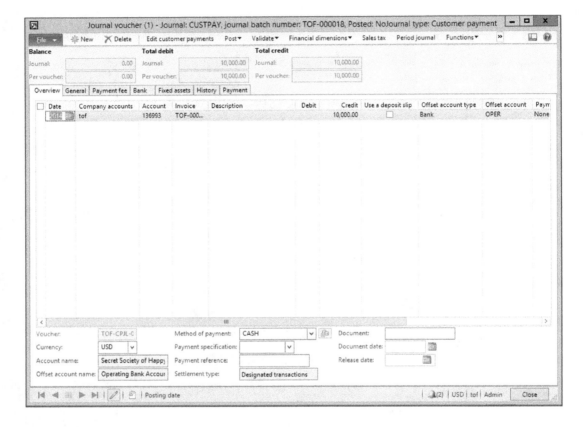

In this case the Invoice was for $10,000, but the customer only paid $9,000.

Entering Customer Payments With Deductions

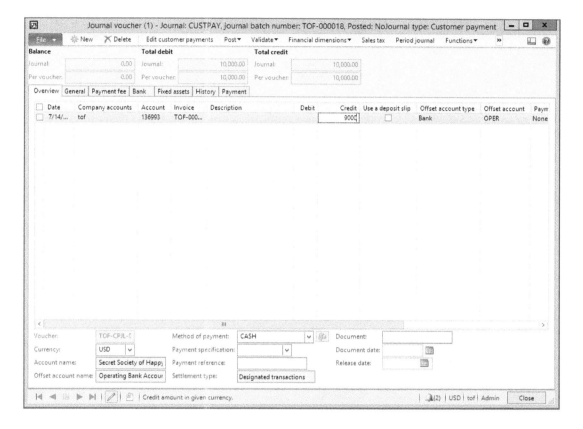

Adjust the credit amount on the Invoice to be the amount that the customer paid.

Entering Customer Payments With Deductions

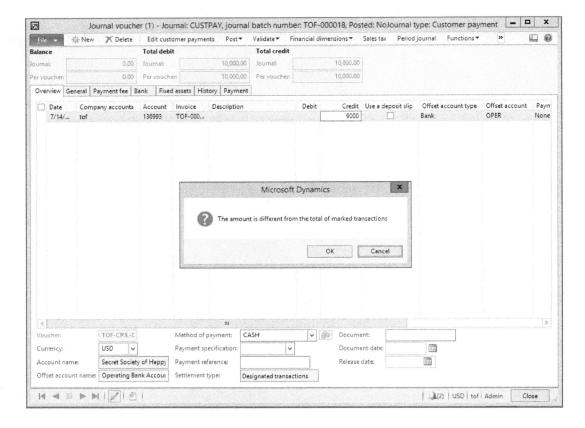

You will get a warning that the invoice is a different value from the transaction. Just click **OK** through the dialog.

Entering Customer Payments With Deductions

Now click on the **Deductions** button in the menu bar.

Entering Customer Payments With Deductions

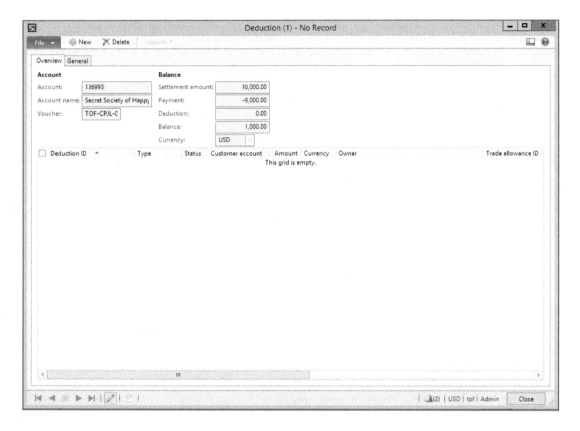

This will open up the **Deductions** maintenance form. Click on the **New** button to add a new record.

Entering Customer Payments With Deductions

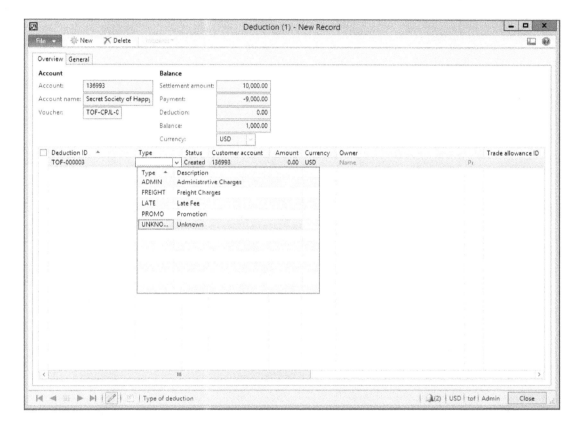

Then select the **Type** of deduction that the customer is claiming.

Entering Customer Payments With Deductions

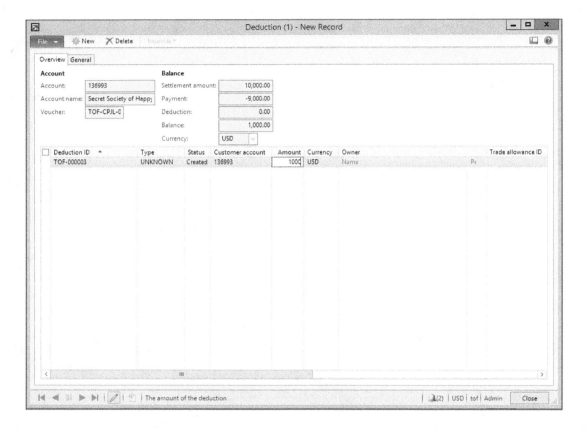

And also update the **Amount** to match the deduction.

Entering Customer Payments With Deductions

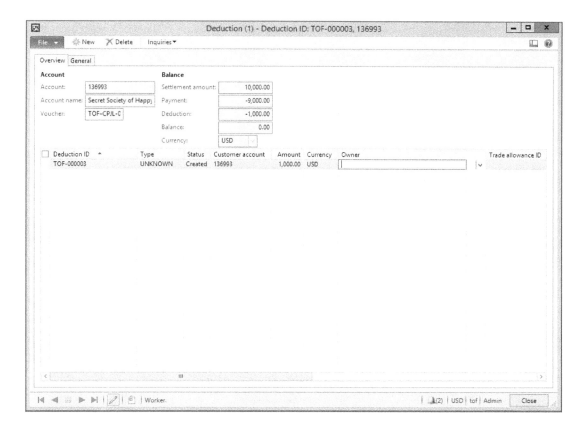

After you have done this, click on the **Close** button to exit from the form.

Entering Customer Payments With Deductions

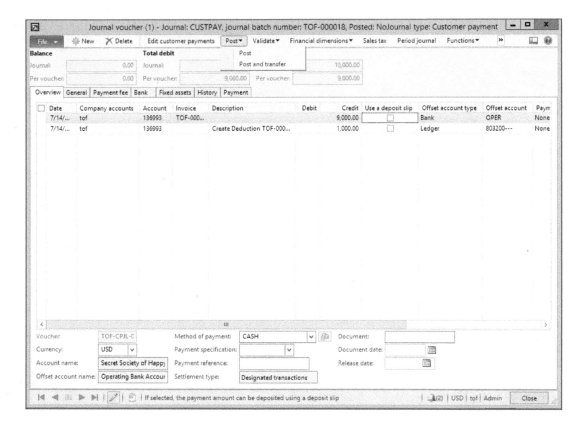

When you return to the **Payment Journal** you will notice that there is an additional line for the deduction and the Journal now matches the offsetting invoice.

All that is left to do is to click on the **Post** menu button and select the **Post** menu item to post the journal to the subledger.

Entering Customer Payments With Deductions

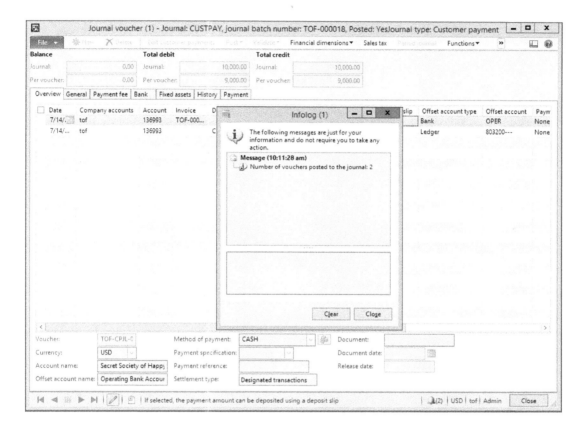

You will then get a notice that a couple of journals have been posted.

Viewing Deductions Through The Deductions Workbench

Once the **Deductions** have been registered within the **Payment Journal** it becomes the task of someone to start investigating the deductions to see if they are valid. For this task, you can use the **Deductions Workbench** that has been designed just for this task.

Viewing Deductions Through The Deductions Workbench

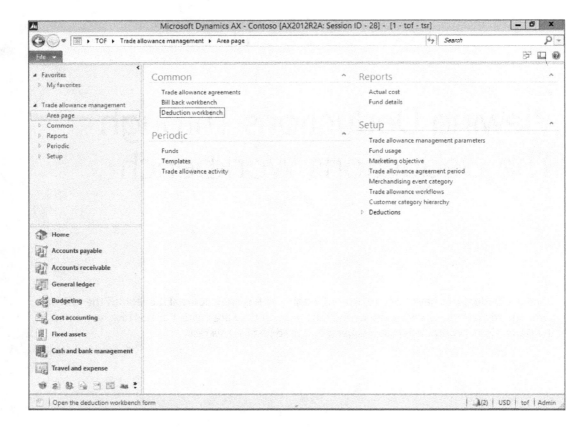

To access this screen click on the **Deductions Workbench** menu item within the **Common** group of the **Trade Allowance Management** area page.

Viewing Deductions Through The Deductions Workbench

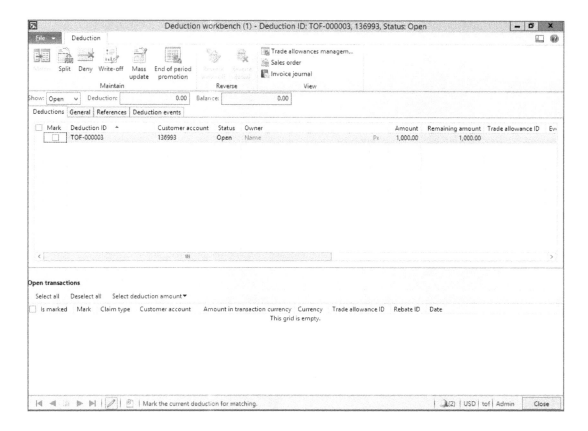

When the **Deduction Workbench** is displayed you will see all of the active deductions that need to be investigated.

Splitting Deductions

As you are investigating **Deductions** you might find that it is really a number of different deductions that need to be treated differently. That's not a problem, because you can split the deductions through the **Deduction Workbench** and then work on the individual items separately.

Splitting Deductions

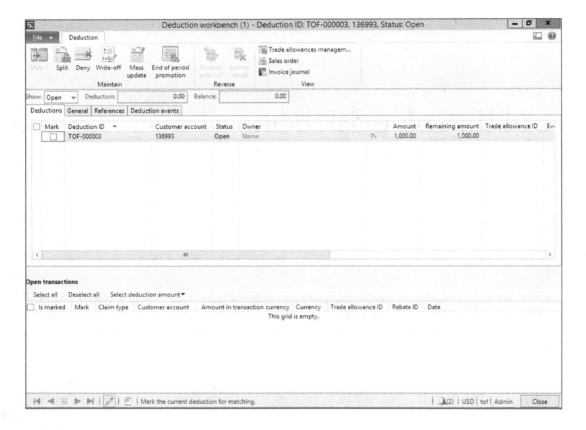

To do this, open up the **Deduction Workbench**, select the deduction that you want to split and click on the **Split** button within the **Maintain** group of the **Deduction** ribbon bar.

Splitting Deductions

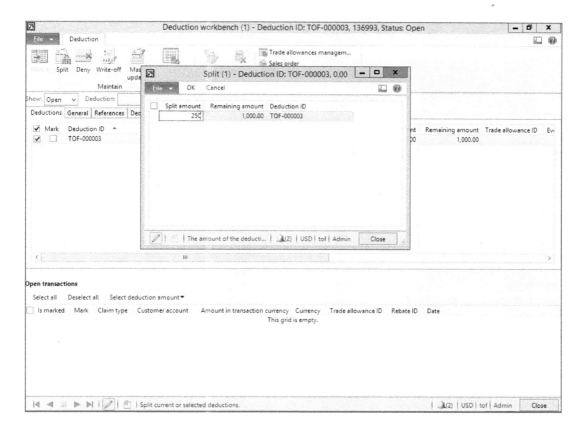

This will open up the **Split** dialog box. All you need to do is type in the amount that you want to create as a new deduction record and then click the **OK** button.

Splitting Deductions

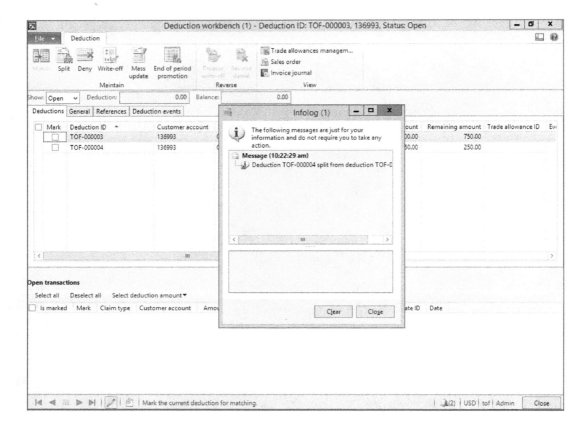

You will get a quick InfoLog message telling you that he split was successful.

Splitting Deductions

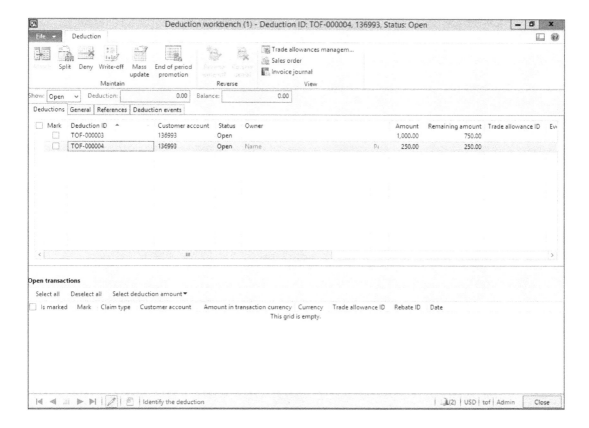

And when you return to the **Deduction Workbench** you will notice that the original deduction has been reduced and there is a new deduction record for the split amount.

Writing Off Deductions

If we find that a deduction is valid then we can write it off directly from the **Deduction Workbench**.

Writing Off Deductions

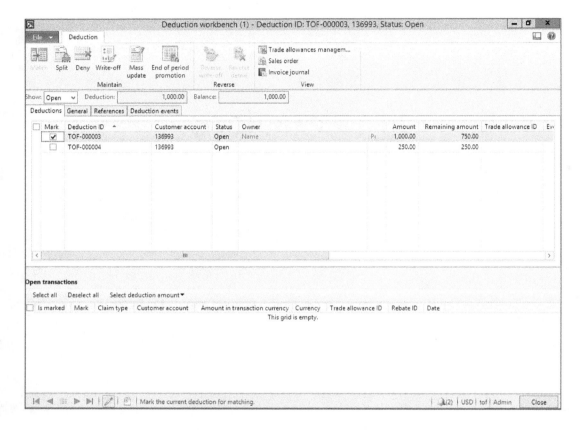

To do this, open up the **Deduction Workbench**, select the **Deduction** that you want to write-off by checking the **Mark** flag and then click on the **Write-Off** button within the **Maintain** group of the **Deduction** ribbon bar.

Writing Off Deductions

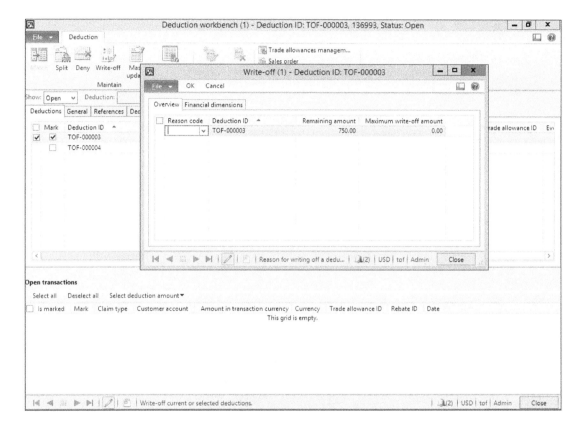

This will open up a **Write-Off** dialog box for you.

Writing Off Deductions

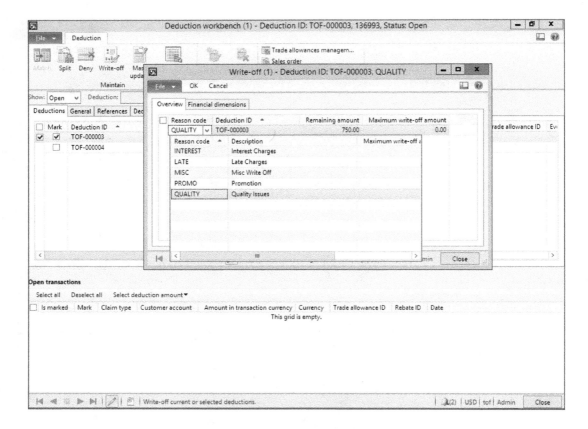

From the **Reason Code** dropdown list, select the reason for the write-off.

Writing Off Deductions

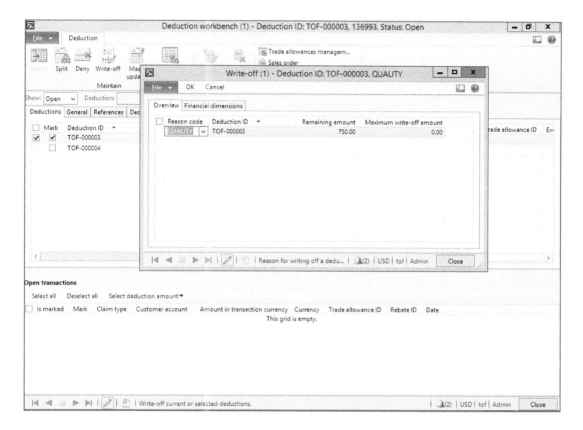

And then click on the **OK** button.

Writing Off Deductions

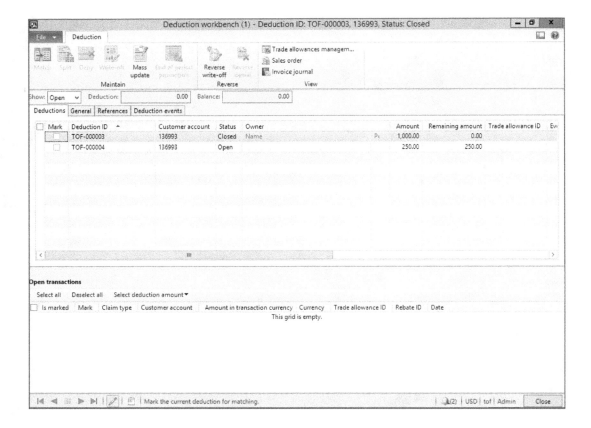

When you return to the **Deduction Workbench** you will notice that the deduction now has a 0 amount remaining and has been cleared.

Denying Deductions

If you don't think that the deduction is valid, then you can return it to the customer's account by denying it within the **Deduction Workbench.**

Denying Deductions

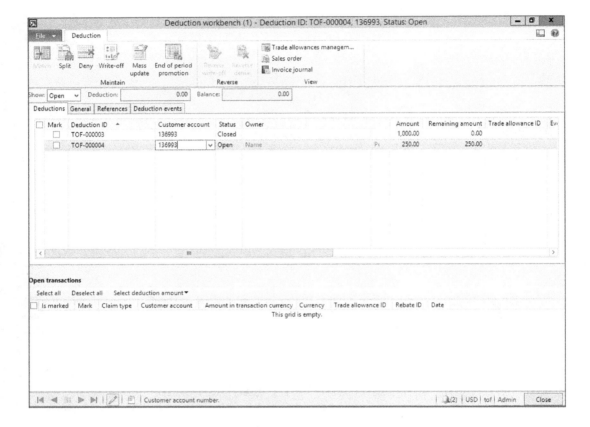

To do this, open up the **Deduction Workbench**, select the **Deduction** that you want to write-off by checking the **Mark** flag and then click on the **Deny** button within the **Maintain** group of the **Deduction** ribbon bar

Denying Deductions

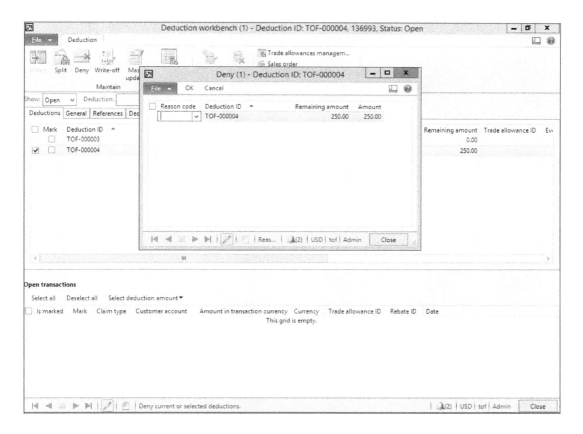

This will open up a **Deny** dialog box for you.

Denying Deductions

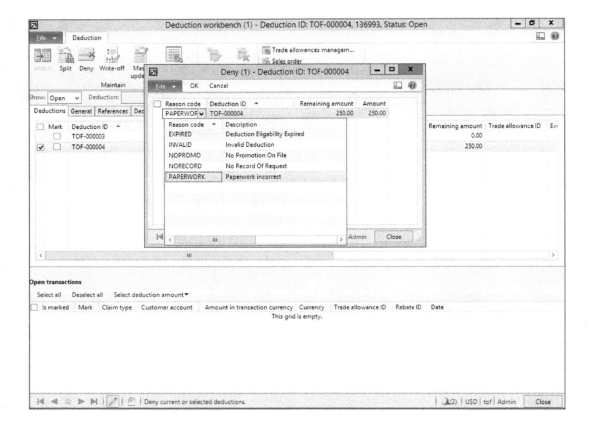

From the **Reason Code** dropdown list, select the reason for the denial.

Denying Deductions

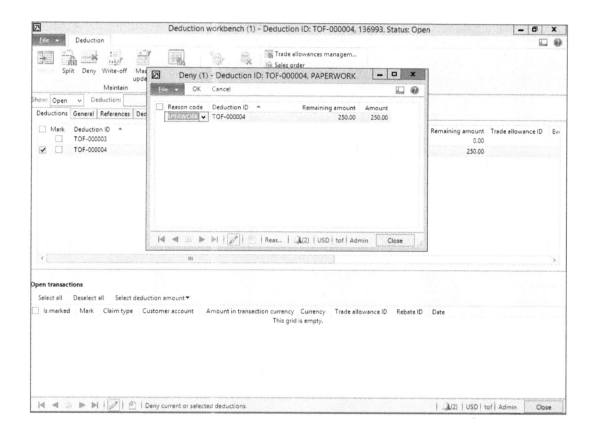

Denying Deductions

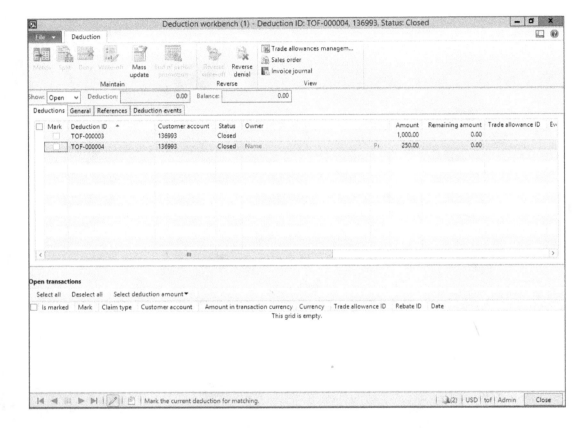

When you return to the **Deduction Workbench** you will notice that the deduction now has a 0 amount remaining and has been cleared.

Denying Deductions

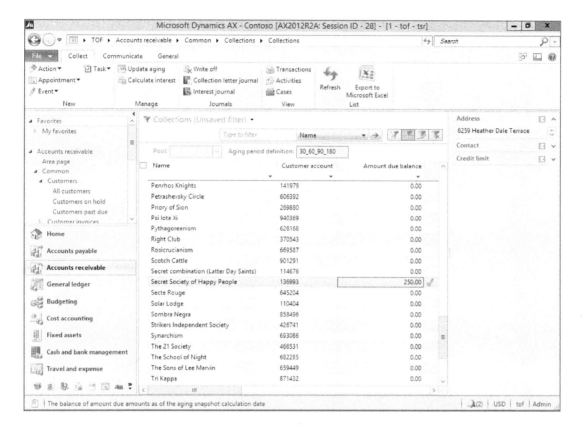

When you view the customer account you will also notice that the deduction amount that you denied is now back on their again.

Now that's useful.

SUMMARY

Hopefully this book has given you a good introduction to the simplest features within Dynamics AX that relate to Accounts Receivable and will have shown you how to start configuring them to be used in your own implementation.

This is just a starting point for you though because there are a lot more features and functions that you may have noticed along the way that you can take advantage of.

Want More Tips & Tricks For Dynamics AX?

The Tips & Tricks series is a compilation of all the cool things that I have found that you can do within Dynamics AX, and are also the basis for my Tips & Tricks presentations that I have been giving for the AXUG, and online. Unfortunately book page size restrictions mean that I can only fit 50 tips & tricks per book, but I will create new volumes every time I reach the 50 Tip mark.

To get all of the details on this series, then here is the link:

http://dynamicsaxcompanions.com/tipsandtricks

Need More Help With Dynamics AX?

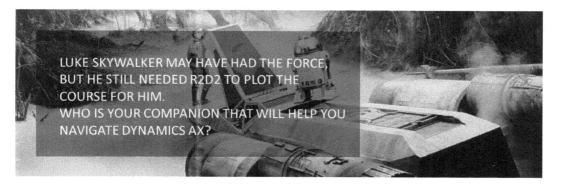

LUKE SKYWALKER MAY HAVE HAD THE FORCE,
BUT HE STILL NEEDED R2D2 TO PLOT THE
COURSE FOR HIM.
WHO IS YOUR COMPANION THAT WILL HELP YOU
NAVIGATE DYNAMICS AX?

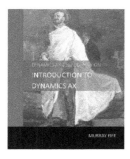

After creating a number of my walkthroughs on SlideShare showing how to configure the different areas within Dynamics AX, I had a lot of requests for the original documents so that people could get a better view of many of the screen shots and also have a easy reference as they worked through the same process within their own systems. To make them easier to access, I am in the process of moving all of the content to the Dynamics AX Companions website to easier access. If you are looking for details on how to configure and use Dynamics AX, then this is a great place for you to start.

Here is the link for the site:

http://dynamicsaxcompanions.com/

About Me

I am an author - I'm no Dan Brown but my books do contain a lot of secret codes and symbols that help guide you through the mysteries of Dynamics AX.

I am a curator - gathering all of the information that I can about Dynamics AX and filing it away within the Dynamics AX Companions archives.

I am a pitchman - I am forever extolling the virtues of Dynamics AX to the unwashed masses convincing them that it is the best ERP system in the world.

I am a Microsoft MVP - this is a big deal, there are less than 10 Dynamics AX MVP's in the US, and less than 30 worldwide.

I am a programmer - I know enough to get around within code, although I leave the hard stuff to the experts so save you all from my uncommented style.

WEB	**www.**murrayfife.me
EMAIL	murray@dynamicsaxcompanions.com
TWITTER	@murrayfife
SKYPE	murrayfife
AMAZON	www.amazon.com/author/murrayfife
WEB	www.dynamicsaxcompanions.com

www.ingramcontent.com/pod-product-compliance
Lightning Source LLC
Chambersburg PA
CBHW080134060326
40689CB00018B/3782